Journey to
Wholeness

The Story, The Tools, The Choice

Larry E. Simons *and*
Carmen DiNino Alspach, LPC, LCDC

WestBow
PRESS
A DIVISION OF THOMAS NELSON

WestBow Press books may be ordered through booksellers or by contacting:

WestBow Press
A Division of Thomas Nelson
1663 Liberty Drive
Bloomington, IN 47403
www.westbowpress.com
1-(866) 928-1240

Because of the dynamic nature of the Internet, any web addresses or links contained in this book may have changed since publication and may no longer be valid. The views expressed in this work are solely those of the author and do not necessarily reflect the views of the publisher, and the publisher hereby disclaims any responsibility for them.

Any people depicted in stock imagery provided by Thinkstock are models, and such images are being used for illustrative purposes only.

Certain stock imagery © Thinkstock.

ISBN: 978-1-4497-2861-8 (sc)
ISBN: 978-1-4497-2862-5 (hc)
ISBN: 978-1-4497-2860-1 (e)
Library of Congress Control Number: 2011918065

Printed in the United States of America

WestBow Press rev. date: 10/17/2011

CONTENTS

BOOK DISCLAIMER

This book is based on the research and personal experience of the authors. The information contained herein is not intended to replace any necessary therapy from mental health professionals. It is simply one man's story and the tools and strategies that worked in his particular case.

This information is intended solely for educational and informational purposes and is not intended as medical or psychological advice. Please consult a medical or mental health professional if you have questions about your mental health. No patent liability is assumed with respect to the use of the information contained herein. Although every precaution has been taken in the preparation of this book, the publisher and the authors assume no responsibility for errors or omissions. Neither is any liability assumed for damages resulting from the information contained herein.

To Cammie

A gift of love

PREFACE

Larry

By profession I am a salesman. I realized at a fairly early age that if I was not going to be a doctor or a lawyer, I had better learn to sell something and I had better get good at it. I am a professional salesman and I have enjoyed a wonderful professional life.

I have found many tools through the years that have helped me be successful both as a salesman and in life. These same tools have also helped me on this journey.

Carmen was my counselor. I met her about a month after the greatest tragedy of my life. She has become one of the most trusted and cherished people I have ever known. What a gift! We started on a journey together. She has been, and still continues on this journey with me. She has proven to be a wonderful traveling partner. She has helped me find joy again. She has helped me find peace. She enabled me to be made whole again.

This story, this journey starts with one of life's most tragic events, then another tragic event, then another and then the one tragic event that I could have let destroy my life. This type of tragedy has destroyed many lives and many marriages. How did I, how does anyone survive in a world with so much pain and tragedy? How do you find joy again?

You might ask where this journey is taking us. How long is the journey going to be? When and how do we start and how do we know when we are at the journey's end? These are all great questions to ask, questions we will answer.

I want to share with you how I found joy again, great joy. I want to share with you how I not only made it back, but made it back better than when the journey started. I want to share some ideas, some thoughts, some experiences and some tools that I used on my journey.

My most sincere prayer is that this book can and will help you on your life's journey.

Come with us on a journey, a journey to wholeness!

PREFACE

Carmen

Welcome to healing. Welcome to hope. Welcome to recovery.

There is a Taoist story about an old farmer who had worked his crops for many years. One day his horse ran away. Upon hearing the news, his neighbors came to visit. "Such bad luck," they said sympathetically. "May be," the farmer replied.

The next morning the horse returned, bringing with it three other wild horses. "How wonderful," the neighbors exclaimed. "May be," replied the old man.

The following day, his son tried to ride one of the untamed horses, was thrown, and broke his leg. The neighbors again came to offer their sympathy on his misfortune. "May be," answered the farmer.

The day after, military officials came to the village to draft young men into the army. Seeing that the son's leg was broken, they passed him by. The neighbors congratulated the farmer on how well things had turned out. "May be," said the farmer.

This story, like our story, reminds us that things are not always as they seem in the beginning and that some things which seem negative can turn out to be wonderful gifts in the end.

People often ask if there can truly be healing following horrific trauma and loss. The answer is a resounding yes and the good news is that there is a choice and the choice is ours to make.

People ask, "What is the secret?" The secret is that that we all have the incredible power to choose to focus on the tragedy and the pain of our loss or to shift our focus and make the choice to primarily concentrate on the blessings and beautiful memories we have of our loved ones. The choice we make could very well be the most critical one of our lives.

Our book is the best of the gifts that Larry and I have received in our lifetimes. Nothing could make us happier than to share these gifts with you.

ACKNOWLEDGMENTS

Larry

The problem with acknowledging people is that you just can't thank everyone and there is no way to miss thanking some people. With that being said, I want each and every person who has been with me, stood beside me, loved me, supported me, held me up, and encouraged me on this journey to know how much I love and appreciate you. I must list a few people who have made significant contributions.

- Fran Moss for being my guardian angel.
- Mary-Lynn Polk, the first to read our manuscript and encourage us.
- A special thank you to Joe Navarro for his love, encouragement, support, and for giving me a time and a place to heal.
- Alan Loibl for all of his help with the layout of the book.
- Hugh Robertson for his marketing expertise.
- Kay Coulter for her kind and loving care in editing our book.
- Rick Alspach for loaning me his wife for so many hours as my counselor and then the hundreds of hours and late nights writing the book.
- Reverend Merrill Wade and Reverend Susan Barnes, my priests, for love, support, spiritual guidance, and sage advice.
- Our St Matthews Episcopal Church extended family.
- Carmen Alspach for being with and supporting me through this latest journey in my life, through a river of tears and the countless hours as my counselor. Once the counseling

relationship ended Carmen accepted my offer to fill a new role as co-author of this book.

- And last but certainly not least, my beautiful and precious wife of thirty-nine years, Debbie. You have always been there for me. You have supported and encouraged me through the good and the bad times. You held me up when I could not stand alone. You are the wind beneath my wings. I love you with all my heart. You are the love of my life.

ACKNOWLEDGMENTS

Carmen

To my beloved husband, Rick Alspach, thank you for the tremendous support, love, encouragement, and spirituality I have been blessed to receive from you. Thank you from the bottom of my heart for always sharing your experience, strength, hope, and time with me throughout this writing process and for always believing in me.

Thank you, Debbie Simons, for sharing your home, your hospitality, and your great courage and strength with me during the writing of *The Journey to Wholeness*. You are a blessing in my life and in the lives of many.

Thank you, Larry Simons, for inviting me to be a part of the most sacred journey of all, your journey to wholeness. Thank you for the opportunity to work with you to honor Cammie. It has been a privilege to walk beside you and to witness your restoration and recovery.

Heartfelt thanks to two beautiful angels, Dr. Mary Lou Boone Clayton and Mary Elizabeth Clayton, for your constant love, encouragement, support, and belief in me throughout my lifetime. Thank you for your constant reminders that this life-saving information must be shared with others.

Thank you, Cathy Collins, for your constant belief, support, kindness, and encouragement in good times and in bad and in sickness and in health. Thank you for your loyalty and for your beautiful spirit.

Thank you to the most beautiful angel of all, Cammie, for inspiring your father to embark on his journey to wholeness and for allowing me to know the gift that you are. Thank you for the opportunity to witness your father's transformation and for carrying your message to others.

PART ONE

JOURNEY

to

WHOLENESS

THE STORY

CHAPTER 1

UTOPIA
Larry

"Sometimes I wish I were a little kid again; skinned
knees are easier to fix than broken hearts."
Author unknown

What is Utopia like? Many people have asked that question. Utopia
for most people is a mythical place, a place of mythical perfection.
For me, Utopia was a real place that was perfect, a place that time
had almost forgotten, a small hamlet about seventy-five miles west
of San Antonio, Texas. My first memories in life are of Utopia, that
small town in the Texas Hill Country. It would remind you of the city
in the movie, *Dancer Texas Population 81*. The difference between
Dancer and Utopia is that the population of Utopia was about 175 in
the early 1950s.

Utopia was a great place to be a little boy. There was an innocence
about this place. The town had a small café, a filling station, and a Red
& White Grocery. Life was good. We lived in a small frame house
with a windmill to pump our water. We had a washing machine, but
the clothes were hung on the clothesline outside to dry. Nothing smells
better than sheets that have dried in the fresh air on a clothesline. I
had a goat named Billy who disappeared one day after eating literally
everything in our yard and part of the interior of our car. To this day
no one remembers what happened to Billy. I think I know . . .

My first memories start when I was about four years old. I lived with my mother Vera, my father Vernon, and my big brother Leroy. Financially life was tough in Utopia for our family. My dad owned and ran the cedar yard on the edge of town. A cedar yard is neatly stacked piles of different sizes of cedar posts. The posts were used for fencing by ranchers all over the state. My dad would work a crew of men in the cedar brakes. This was in the days before chain saws and the posts were cut with a double-bladed ax. To say it was a tough way to make a living is an understatement. By today's standards, I was born into relative poverty. I did not realize what a great benefit was until much later in life. Although life was a struggle for my family financially, there was always food on the table and gifts at Christmas and birthdays. For this four-year-old boy it truly was Utopia.

I had several aunts, uncles, and cousins who lived in Utopia. Everybody knew everyone and everything about everyone in town. I remember playing with my cousins and gathering eggs for the elderly couple that lived across the street. Their chicken coop was behind their very small house. I still remember the first time they fixed fried doves and how wonderful it tasted. The hearth of the fireplace in their home was even with the floor, not a raised hearth like we are accustomed to seeing today. That fireplace was so inviting that my wife Debbie and I decided to design and build that same type of hearth and fireplace in the same vintage style in our current home. I remember making kites out of dried sunflower stalks, flour and water paste, and newspapers. I remember Vacation Bible School at the Baptist church in the summer. I remember the rodeo parade in the summer before the rodeo in July. Life was simple. Life was good for this four-year-old boy. It truly was Utopia; it truly was perfect.

CHAPTER 2

HUMBLE BEGINNINGS

Carmen

"A human life is a story told by God."
Hans Christian Andersen

Larry had a very idyllic early childhood, which gave him a stable start in life with simple, wholesome values, an intact family of origin and close family relationships. This stable foundation, although early in life, would prove to be a critical element in his stability and resiliency and would be the strong foundation from which he would weather the future storms ahead. It would be the last time he experienced anything resembling a utopian period in his life.

It cannot be stated strongly enough how important a role a stable childhood can have on a person. Oftentimes a stable early life, especially one of modest means, can be taken for granted, minimized, or even seen as something less than an asset. However, in Larry's case, the years of growing up in a small Texas town in the 1950s would be the solid foundation upon which he would build a prosperous and successful life. This foundation would be tested and shaken to the core. It would be tested so severely that cracks would eventually occur. But Larry's values, his strength, and his roots would be firmly grounded in this foundation. A child with a shallower root system, less grounding, or less stability would find it all but impossible to weather the tumultuous storms ahead. Larry would come to view early childhood as a time from which he would draw great strength.

When our lives become extremely stressful, human beings often cope by reverting to what is familiar, back to what has worked in the past, or back to their core values. If we do not have a firm foundation from our childhoods, we have to create one and do the best we can. A firm foundation cannot be created quickly, it can only be created by experience and takes time to develop. Rocky foundations are developed in haste, in a short period of time, and can never be truly firm.

Larry's strong foundation would turn out to be one of the most stabilizing factors in his later life. It would turn out to be a great blessing and something about which he would have much gratitude.

CHAPTER 3

LEAVING UTOPIA

Larry

"What lies behind us and what lies before us are tiny matters
compared to what lies within us."
Ralph Waldo Emerson

Just before my sixth birthday in 1955, we moved from Utopia to
Austin, Texas, the place of my birth and home of most of my relatives,
including both sets of grandparents. We moved into an area of town
called Govalle, on the east side of Austin. I started elementary school
and Leroy, my older brother, started junior high school. Life for me
was still simple.

Kay Street where we lived was still a dirt road, but I didn't think
this was odd because all the streets in Utopia were dirt roads except
for the main road through town. Kay Street was paved several years
after we moved into the neighborhood.

I had many friends in the neighborhood and at school. Gene
Schneider and I met when I was six and Gene was seven. We are still
friends today. I have many fond memories of our times together.

Dad opened a salvage yard on East 1st Street. I have many fond
childhood memories of doing odd jobs around the salvage yard for
Dad, who taught me the value of a dollar and what hard work was
all about.

When I was in the third grade we moved to New Mexico for about a year. Dad had a bailing machine that turned junk cars into cubes of crushed metal which were then hauled to the steel mills. After living in three different locations of New Mexico that year, we moved back to Austin. Unfortunately, Dad's bailing machine idea was about fifty years too soon. In today's economy he would have made a fortune with that bailing machine.

When we moved back to Austin, Dad opened a business in Round Rock, Texas called Texas Pipe and Salvage. I loved that place and continued to do odd jobs for my dad. Occasionally I would get to go on a trip with him in his eighteen-wheeler. What fond memories I have of when life was simple, when life was innocent.

CHAPTER 4

A FATHER'S LEGACY

Carmen

"Preach the gospel as loudly as you can, and,
if you have to, use words."
Saint Francis of Assisi

Larry's father gave him three critical gifts at this time. His dad gave him the gift of learning about and practicing a strong work ethic when his son was just a little boy. The second gift was learning about and understanding the value of money. The third gift was the experience of feeling love, quality time, and security from a caring, strong, and honorable father.

Parents are often our first teachers and Larry's father taught him well by example. His dad did not just tell him about hard work and the benefits that come as a result, he also let Larry see him working hard and also let Larry participate with him in the work he did. Larry was taught in an apprentice style of learning. Larry learned by watching the man under whom he was apprenticing and by working alongside his father and practicing the skills his father imparted to him.

Kids today typically do not have the opportunity to learn about the value of money at an early age because times and values are significantly different now than they were back in the 1950s. Back in the 1950s Larry and many other children of that era did not have spending money given to them by their parents. At that time, working and doing important tasks for their parents or for their family members was the way children earned their spending money. If no work was done, there was no spending money. Larry's father had given him the gift of yearning for something special, working hard to purchase it, delaying his gratification until the money was earned, and then enjoying the fruits of his labor. Larry's father's legacy to him was learning about the honor and value of work and the value of money. Larry had fun learning these important lessons alongside his father. These two lessons would be some of the most valuable lessons of his life and would enable Larry to build a very lucrative career and to have the skills necessary to survive the trials ahead of him.

Other valuable gifts Larry's dad left him were the gifts of time, love, and security. No amount of money could have purchased these priceless gifts for Larry and he was a quick, appreciative, and dedicated student. These specific gifts his father left his son would be the sturdy base upon which Larry would build his life and the base upon which he would weather all future storms.

Because Larry's father demonstrated through his actions how to be a caring, strong, and honorable man to his son and to his family, Larry learned to be caring, strong, and honorable too. Children learn what they live and experience and Larry's father was an excellent teacher. His son learned these lessons so well that he acquired these values and made them a permanent part of his own character.

CHAPTER 5

LOST CHILDHOOD
Larry

"There are things that we don't want to happen but have to accept,
things we don't want to know but have to learn, and people we
can't live without but have to let go."
Author unknown

On a Wednesday evening in April of 1960, I was ten years old and
had been playing at my friend Gene Schneider's house on the next
block. At about 6:00 or 6:30 in the evening I decided to go home. My
mother had gone to church and my brother Leroy was gone as well,
but Dad was supposed to be home. I walked into the house and called
out to Dad, but no one answered. I walked down the hall and heard
a strange gurgling sound coming from the bathroom, a sound I will
never forget. I called out to Dad again and still no answer. I tried to
push the door open, but there was something against it. I pushed my
way into the bathroom to find my father lying on the floor in a pool
of blood with a rifle lying beside him and a bullet wound between his
eyes. I ran screaming to the next door neighbor's house. The neighbor
went to verify my story. He came back and called the police and I
heard a word I had never heard before, when the neighbor told the
police there had been a homicide.

The events for the balance of that night are sketchy. I remember
being taken to a friend's house for a while and then being taken to

the hospital. Later that evening I went to my grandmother's house to spend the night. In the morning when I woke up, one of my dad's brothers, my favorite uncle on that side of the family, Uncle Ed, told me that my father had gone to heaven. Homicide, suicide, I did not know the difference, but I would find out on my own in the coming days what suicide meant.

My mother had a nervous breakdown and my father's suicide was never discussed, even to this day. The elephant is still in the living room. You see, in 1960, suicide was not something you talked about. It was something to be ashamed of. I had nightmares, but the events of my father's death were still never discussed. I can still see the events of the evening I found my father. They are still as clear in my mind as if it happened yesterday. I had feelings of abandonment, feelings of guilt. I felt for a long time that I was going to be an orphan. I was afraid that Mother was going to die also and I didn't know where I would end up. At times I felt so alone. There was no one I could talk to about my father's death. Suicide was a taboo subject that was not discussed, especially with a child. No adult in my life would mention a word about the fact that my father's death was a suicide. I think the feeling was that time would heal all wounds; at least that's what I was told.

I remember going back to school after my father's death. No one would talk to me about it, not even my teacher. It was a taboo subject. I do remember one boy telling me that my father had gone to hell because he committed suicide. That discussion ended in a fight.

Later that summer, my sixteen-year-old brother Leroy eloped, leaving my mother and me alone. I really felt abandoned then. My brother, whom I idolized, was gone, leaving me alone with Mother. I spent a lot of time with my maternal grandparents and a maternal aunt. I loved these people very much, but talking about my father's death was not permitted.

We tried continuing to live in that house where Dad had died, but after a while Mom leased the house to someone else. We then moved into a house in San Antonio that had been converted into four apartments. We lived with old friends from Utopia. What a difficult time this was for me. I had lost my father to suicide, my brother had eloped, and we had moved away from my home, my friends, and my school. I was lost. I was able to make a few friends, but school was difficult.

After being in San Antonio for only six months, we returned to Austin. For a while we lived in a small house that our family owned. Later we moved into a duplex and I went back to school in my old neighborhood.

My father had been dead three years and I was thirteen years old when my mother married a fine man named Alden. I became very fond of him. When my mother asked me how I felt about her marrying him, I told her that, although I liked him a lot, one thing would never change—I would always be my father's son. When I was sixteen, I too eloped to marry my high school sweetheart. My first child was born one month after my seventeenth birthday, a little girl, Dawn Michelle. Two years later, my second daughter, Cammie, was born. Three years later the marriage ended in divorce, with my ex-wife getting custody of both children.

CHAPTER 6

COPING

Carmen

"Earth has no sorrow that heaven cannot heal."
Author unknown

The shock and horror of finding the body and experiencing the suicidal death of his beloved father was a trauma that any little boy would have difficulty surviving. To compound the effect, the lack of any family communication regarding this monumental loss would create incredible emotional distance between Larry and his family members. This distance within the family created isolation, fear, terror, confusion, insecurity, and a tremendous feeling of loss of control in the life of ten-year-old Larry. Unaddressed and unprocessed, these feelings would haunt and stay within Larry for years to come.

Larry began experiencing some of the Seven Stages of Grief immediately following his discovery of his father's body. Larry experienced Shock and Denial, Pain and Guilt, Anger and Bargaining, and Depression and Loneliness. This was a tremendous load, a tremendous burden for a ten-year-old boy to carry alone. It would be several years before Larry could work through the remaining stages, The Upward Turn, Reconstruction, and Working Through and Acceptance and Hope.

In those days the stages of grief were not known and were not discussed, so Larry did not have the words to describe what was happening to him. Larry did not know that he was going through the first stage of grief known as Shock and Denial. A little boy's mind does not have the experience or maturity to conceive of the fact that his father could die so suddenly, much less die so violently and by his own hand, and so the shock and denial stage served the purpose of cushioning the blow of this devastating turn of events. Larry looked at his situation with numbed disbelief and at first denied the reality of the death of his father in order to avoid the pain. He thought, *This cannot be happening to me.* Shock provided emotional protection from the full knowledge of the death and from being overwhelmed with this information all at once.

Feelings of abandonment from the death of his father, the emotional unavailability of his mother, and the departure of his older brother to teen marriage left Larry alone to survive and navigate the complexities of life. Pressures of this magnitude take away the ability of children to just be children, and Larry was no exception.

Human beings can only tolerate emotional distance from significant others in their lives for so long. When the distance becomes too great, too intolerable, human beings are designed to automatically seek closeness wherever they can for purposes of survival. Larry had the resilience and emotional strength to tolerate the vast distance in his life for six years following the suicide of his father. At the tender age of sixteen, the distance finally became intolerable and Larry found closeness the only way he could. Closeness came in the form of a high school sweetheart. Since he could not find adequate closeness in his family of origin, Larry predictably created family closeness one of the few ways available to a teen, dropping out of school, marrying his girlfriend at the age of sixteen, and having his first child by the age seventeen. Miraculously, Larry had created the family he needed to survive.

Given the possible options and alternatives that could have been used as coping mechanisms such as alcohol, drugs, behavioral rebellion, or suicide, Larry made the best survival decisions a hurting, grieving, wounded, and neglected sixteen-year-old could. Given the alternatives, it is understandable and easy to see that marriage was the least detrimental option available to him at that time. This option did work, but only for a brief period of time. Although the decision to marry and have children did meet some of Larry's emotional needs initially, it still was a decision made impulsively with a teenager's level of maturity and was not the answer to his mounting levels of anxiety and profound grief.

Even though Larry cared for his wife, adored his daughters, and took full responsibility for their support, the match was not sustainable. The loss of custody of his children, a very common occurrence for fathers at that time, was another devastating and heartbreaking loss Larry had to endure.

By the age of twenty one, Larry had lost his father to suicide, his family of origin to grief and loss, his wife to divorce, and his children to a custody ruling. Unfortunately, this was only the beginning of the staggering losses Larry would have to endure. Sometimes it is very difficult to understand how much loss a person can tolerate. Sometimes it is difficult to see light in the darkness.

CHAPTER 7

STARTING OVER

Larry

"God grant me the serenity
To accept the things I cannot change;
Courage to change the things I can;
And wisdom to know the difference."
Reinhold Niebuhr

In 1972 I met a wonderful young lady and fell in love. We were inseparable. Debbie accepted and loved my two daughters as if they were her own.

In the spring of 1972, not long after Debbie and I met, I received a phone call that my favorite uncle on Mother's side of the family had committed suicide. Uncle Hunter's death was very similar to my father's. Uncle Hunter had been like a brother to my father and a second father to me. I loved my uncle so much. He left behind a wife, a teenage son, and a daughter. He left behind a lot of broken hearts including mine.

Uncle Hunter was a master welder and taught me how to weld. He could create just about anything out of a piece of metal. I worked with him for a while at Modern Supply Machine Shop in Austin. I was seventeen years old, just a kid myself, with a kid of my own, working to support my new family. Uncle Hunter convinced the owners to hire me, and I worked under his strict supervision and will never forget that experience. I treasured my time with him and still have the tools I used when we worked together. Those tools have my initials welded on the handles. Whenever I use one, even to this day, I think about the wonderful times we had. Uncle Hunter was an important person in my life. He was a gift.

In December, 1972, Debbie and I married. This was and continues to be a loving and stable relationship. Dawn and Cammie came for frequent visits. After we had been married for five years, my youngest daughter Cammie came to live with Debbie and me. Cammie had come to Austin to spend some time with us in the summer of 1977 and I remember asking Cammie, then nine years old, when she would have to go home? How long would she be able to stay with Debbie and me? She informed me that she was home and that she was not going back to live with her mother and stepfather. At this point a new chapter of our life began with a nine-year-old little girl living with us on a permanent basis, and life was good for our family.

I will never forget stopping at the grocery store one day and going in to get an item or two. Debbie and Cammie remained in the car while I went inside. When I returned I could tell that Debbie had been crying. I asked what had been going on. Debbie said we just needed to go home. When we got home, and I had a moment alone with Deb, she revealed what had transpired in the car. Cammie had asked Debbie if it was ok to call her "Mom." Cammie still called her Debbie most of the time, but always referred to her as "Mom". Debbie truly became her mother and Cammie her daughter. My other daughter, Dawn, chose to continue living with her mother and stepfather and new half brother and sister.

The three of us enjoyed a wonderful life together, camping and boating on the weekends, going on family vacations, and attending school activities. Cammie joined the school band, took private lessons and was an outstanding flutist. She won gold medals for solo and ensemble at the state UIL competition. Debbie and I were presidents of the band booster club during Cammie's junior and senior year in high school.

Cammie's first car was a candy apple red 1967 mustang that she helped me rebuild. We replaced a fender, filled in some rust spots with body filler and sanded it before it was painted. We had a rebuilt engine installed and we installed a new interior. She loved that car and I have to admit so did I.

During Cammie's senior year in high school, I received a phone call from my mother, concerned that she could not find my stepfather. A few minutes later, a neighbor of hers called me to say that my stepfather had committed suicide. Alden had gone into a storage shed in the backyard and shot himself. Alden was a great stepfather. I knew he loved me and I loved him. Dawn and Cammie loved Alden very much. He was their grandfather. He was the only grandfather on my side of the family they ever knew. Since Cammie lived with Debbie and me she saw a lot more of Alden. They became very close. I remember a time when someone told Cammie that Alden was not her "real" grandfather. For Cammie those were fighting words. In her eyes he was her "real" grandfather and she loved him dearly. We had many great times together.

Alden had been in physical pain for several years. After his death, I spent several days with my mother trying to help her put the pieces of her life back together and figuring out where she was financially. Up to this point in my life I had been under the impression that my mother had a pretty good business head on her shoulders. I could not have been further from the truth. Mother was lost and needed help. I helped her get everything put in order and started an investment program for her.

Mother and Cammie were close and became even closer after Alden's death. Cammie's other close confidant was Rena, Debbie's mother. Rena and Houghton, my mother-in-law and father-in-law, loved both of the girls but because Cammie lived with us, she spent a lot more time with them. They were wonderful grandparents. Cammie and Rena became very close and I don't think there was anything that Cammie would not share with Rena. Cammie would spend time with Rena and Houghton on her summer vacations. Rena would take Cammie swimming and indulge her in much too much chocolate and ice cream. They had a very special relationship. Rena was a perfect grandmother and also a perfect mother-in-law to me.

Rena and Houghton were very special to me. After several years as a family, I always referred to them as Mom and Dad. We saw them often and had many wonderful times and holidays together. Deb and her mother talked almost every day. Mom, Rena, died from lung cancer in 1982. It was a tremendous blow to all of us but especially Debbie. She and her mom were so close. Debbie hadn't just lost her mother; she had lost one of her best friends, one of her closest confidants, her sounding board.

Dad, Houghton lived for another thirteen years after Rena died. He lived alone in the same home where they had lived together, the same home where Debbie was raised. We would see Dad every Sunday evening at six o'clock. He was very prompt. We would pick him up for dinner or he would have dinner with us at our home. He died very quickly after being diagnosed with liver cancer, another great loss for all of us. I loved him dearly. I miss him often.

CHAPTER 8

LIFE IS DIFFICULT
Carmen

"There is a time for everything, and a season for every activity under heaven, a time to be born and a time to die, . . . a time to weep and time to laugh, a time to mourn and a time to dance."
Ecclesiastes 3:1-4 NIV

Sometimes Larry began to see light in the darkness. Larry worked hard to earn a living and support his children and blessings came in the form of a beautiful woman named Debbie who became his wife. Larry's career began to flourish and great joy overshadowed the grief in his life. However, in the midst of the joy, another unbelievable loss by suicide occurred. Larry's beloved uncle, a man who was like a second father to Larry, committed suicide. It was almost too much to believe, that a second suicide hit their family and so soon behind the death of Larry's father.

Even though this was another huge loss for Larry, he now had the incredible support of Debbie, and then a few years later the miraculous return of the "apple of his eye," his daughter Cammie. Larry finally had the close, loving family he had dreamed of having since he was a child. Living life with Debbie and Cammie was even better than he had dreamed about.

The deaths of his father and uncle by suicide were very disturbing and generated many questions about life and death for Larry. Why?

Why? Why? Larry was experiencing some of the greatest joy of his life in his new marriage with Debbie, and at the same time, experiencing the death by suicide of another beloved family member. As author Scott Peck once wrote, "Life is difficult," and Larry would learn the skill of experiencing the joys and traumas of life simultaneously. This would be one skill that Larry would have a chance to master, one that would help him survive the trials ahead.

With the support of his beloved wife, Debbie, Larry was able to go through some of the stages of grief by talking about the suicide of his uncle with Debbie. Although Larry and Debbie still did not have the knowledge about the stages of grief, Larry was at least able to begin talking about his experience of loss with Debbie. "I cannot believe this is happening again. Surely my uncle did not kill himself, surely this is a mistake. Something this devastating cannot happen to the same family twice."

Larry also experienced the stage of PAIN and discussed with Debbie how much this hurt to lose another beloved person in his family. "What did our family do to deserve these two deaths by suicide? My life feels out of control, scary, and unpredictable because I have no control over these suicidal deaths in my family, and they happen without warning."

Larry also experienced the stage of Anger and Bargaining and found himself inadvertently bargaining with God saying, "If I promise to be very good perhaps these suicides will stop happening in my family." Alternately Larry found himself saying, "It is not fair that my family should be hit twice by suicide; I know we didn't do anything bad enough to warrant this. How could God allow this to happen?"

CHAPTER 9

THANK HEAVEN FOR LITTLE GIRLS
Larry

"Things are not always what they seem; the first appearance
deceives many; the intelligence of a few perceives what has been
carefully hidden."
Phaedrus

Cammie graduated from high school and attended Southwest Texas
State University. She enjoyed college life very much. Cammie's first
year at Southwest Texas she majored in "party."

Cammie had done an internship her senior year in high school
at the Capitol Area Rehabilitation Center, working with young
children with Cerebral Palsy. She loved children very much. When
she started college her major was physical therapy, but she changed
majors in her sophomore year. Cammie received her Bachelor's
Degree in Elementary Education and teaching certificate in Special
Education.

After graduating from college, Cammie began teaching special
education at an elementary school in San Marcos. Soon after that,
Cammie was married. Cammie had an incredible work ethic. She
could out-work most women or men that I ever met. Unfortunately
her new husband had no work ethic and this created problems in the
marriage and our family. After being married for five years Cammie
ended up on our doorstep one night. She said she was sorry for what

she had put the family through and needed our help. I helped her get a new vehicle and set up in an apartment in San Marcos. The marriage ended in divorce.

Cammie continued teaching school in San Marcos. My mother, who at that time lived in Rockdale, introduced Cammie to her pastor's son. The romance was short and Cammie became engaged to be married. We gave her a big wedding in Rockdale. Her birth mother and stepfather, along with Cammie's half brother and sister came down from Montana for the wedding. After the wedding, she moved to Rockdale and continued teaching Special Ed. A couple of years later she transferred to the Thorndale school district and continued teaching there.

Cammie's life with her new husband seemed to be good. They bought a home and started their life together. Everything seemed quite normal. Cammie very much wanted children but was unable to get pregnant due to a medical condition. She wanted to adopt a child, but after being married for several years, her husband was diagnosed with multiple sclerosis. He obtained medical disability which brought an end to the hope for adoption. In the spring of 2007, Cammie had to have a hysterectomy. The surgery instantly threw her into menopause and all the symptoms that come with it. Her hormones were completely out of balance. Cammie was also being treated for a thyroid condition and that level was out of balance. Cammie was a medical mess. She was taking hormones, thyroid medication, anti-depressant medication, and anti-anxiety medication.

In August we took Cammie and her husband, our other daughter Dawn, and her husband, and our four grandchildren on a family vacation to Concan, Texas. In Concan the big attraction is floating down the Frio River in tubes. This was something Cammie had wanted to do for several years. Cammie seemed fine on this trip and the family had a great vacation together.

CHAPTER 10

LOSING HOPE

Carmen

"Come to me, all who are weary and burdened,
and I will give you rest."
Matthew 11:28

Cammie had a calling to work with children with special needs and was willing to buckle down on her studies in order to get her degree and teaching certification to work with special needs children. Cammie went on to do her life's work of teaching children their academics but was careful to address their emotional needs as well.

While Cammie was headstrong and independent throughout her elementary, middle, high school, and college years, she began to show vulnerability in her decision making especially in regard to romantic relationships. Cammie matured and developed excellent decision making, skills in all areas except choices with regard to marriage. Two decisions, two marriages, these choices would affect her for the remainder of her life in ways she could never have imagined.

Despite these difficult relationships, Cammie was able to grow and excel in her work with children for many years. However, when Cammie sustained several blows that would spin her life out of control, she no longer had coping skills that were adequate enough to deal with these monumental stressors. These stressors included having a complete hysterectomy in her thirties, losing all hope of ever being able to have a child of her own, managing the cocktail of medications prescribed for her depression, anxiety, and thyroid condition, experiencing the dramatic mood swings brought on by the abrupt changes in hormone levels, and unbeknownst to Debbie and Larry, tolerating the escalating abuse in her marriage.

CHAPTER 11

THE DARK DAYS

Larry

"The measure of life is not its duration, but its donation"
Peter Marshall

In September 2007, after only teaching two weeks, Cammie called me to say she was going to resign her teaching position. She told me she could no longer cope with teaching her students. The next day before meeting with me, Cammie met with her principal and took a leave of absence. She then came to meet with me and we talked for several hours. She was tired; she had not slept in several days. She told me her marriage was not working out, but would not go into any details; her whole world was falling apart. She thought her life had been a failure. She was now in her second failed marriage and the career that she loved so much and had given so much to was now too much for her to cope with.

I attempted to get Cammie to come stay with Debbie and me, to give her some time to rest. She went home to gather clothing and personal items and came to our house, but she never made it. She allowed her husband to talk her out of it. About a week later, Cammie went to see her principal again and resigned her teaching position. This incredibly talented young lady who loved teaching, whose students loved her, could not go on any longer.

Once again we attempted to get Cammie to come to Austin, to stay with us again, but she refused. In the later part of September, she called me to inform me that she could not go on living like this; she needed help and needed it now. I asked if she had told her husband and she said he was watching a movie and would take her to the doctor whenever the movie was over. I had Cammie call him to the phone and I convinced him to take her to the doctor immediately. The doctor had her admitted to a psychiatric hospital that night. I visited Cammie everyday, but she would not let Debbie or me be a part of the treatment. She remained in the hospital for about one week before being released. She went back home and was supposed to be in psychotherapy in Rockdale. After only one or two sessions, she discontinued her treatment because of financial pressure at home.

Cammie remained in Rockdale and we talked frequently. She talked about getting a part-time job to have something to do and to help out with their finances. She was getting a lot of pressure at home because she wasn't bringing home a paycheck. Her husband had disability income but Cammie had been the main breadwinner until she resigned her teaching position.

Cammie's world at that time looked like this: Her husband was disabled, had MS and stayed at home all day. She could not have children or adopt children. She had to have a hysterectomy; she was on thyroid medication, anti-depressants, anti-anxiety medication, and hormones. She was in her second failed marriage and had resigned her lifelong career that she loved so much. Cammie's world was upside down and she could not see daylight.

In November 2007, I received another phone call and Cammie was in crisis again. I asked her where her husband was and she informed me that he was outside on the tractor cutting grass. Cammie needed help and needed it then. Her husband walked in the door about that time. When I got him on the phone that time, I informed him he needed to take Cammie to the doctor immediately and if he would not or could not, I would call the Rockdale Police Department to inform them that my daughter was contemplating suicide and they would intervene immediately. He agreed to take Cammie to the doctor and she was again admitted that evening to the psychiatric hospital.

This stay in the hospital was different from the first. Cammie sought out and accepted our support as well as accepting support from the clergy at our church. Cammie opened up to the counselors, doctors, and Debbie and me. She described a verbally and mentally abusive home life that had gone on for years. Debbie and I had had no idea this had been going on. Cammie told us she had threatened to commit suicide a few days before and her husband told her that if she was going to do it, to go outside so she wouldn't make a mess in the house. I was outraged that my son-in-law would speak to my beloved daughter in such a cold, demeaning, insensitive, and dehumanizing way when she was hurting so badly. The doctors recommended that Cammie needed to detach from Rockdale for awhile. We offered Cammie the opportunity to come live with us as long as she needed to, to get her life back in order, to get well. She thanked us and said she felt the weight of the world had been lifted from her shoulders. When she was released from the hospital, she came home to stay with Debbie and me.

She got out of the hospital on a Friday evening and was supposed to start outpatient therapy at the hospital within a week. She also had appointments with a psychiatrist and a psychologist the next week.

The weekend had its high and low points. Cammie got to visit her maternal grandmother, go shopping for some new clothes, and had dinner together. Cammie had not seen very much of her grandparents because, unbeknownst to us, her husband was not fond of them and would not allow her to visit them. On Sunday morning, her whole mood had changed and she was talking about going back to Rockdale. After talking with Debbie and me, Cammie decided to stay. Cammie went to church with us and things seemed fine. On Monday she seemed okay and Cammie wanted something to do around the house while Deb and I went to work. She occupied that day with washing her car, cleaning the back deck, and being with our dog Sophie. That evening after talking to her husband again her whole mood changed.

I got up on Tuesday morning and went upstairs to our workout room for my morning routine. I noticed the door to Cammie's bedroom was ajar, the light was on and the bed had been made. I didn't think much about this because Cammie was an early riser. I went ahead and worked out and when I came out of the workout room in about an hour, the bedroom door was still ajar, but the light was off. I went downstairs and called for Cammie. There was no answer.

I thought she was gone. I looked outside in the driveway and her car was still there. I went back upstairs to check the bedroom and I called out her name. She was sitting in the dark. I asked, "Honey, what are you doing?" And she answered, "Daddy, I'm trying to figure out a way to tell you and Mom that I have to go home." She said, "Daddy; I cannot give up my land, my animals, my house, and my husband. I have to go home." Debbie and I pleaded with her to stay, but you cannot handcuff a thirty-nine-year-old woman to the bed. She had already packed her car and she left for Rockdale.

Cammie's illnesses were depression, chemical imbalance, thyroid imbalance, hormone imbalance, suicidal ideation, and a codependent addiction to her husband.

Later that morning she called me to tell me how much she loved me and to thank me for everything I had done for her. When she hung up with me, she called Debbie and had the same conversation with her. We did not call her that evening. We felt like we needed to give her some space. On Wednesday, November 14, 2007, Debbie and I both went to work. I was leaving later that afternoon for a business trip to Kansas City with my new employer. I had flown from Austin to Dallas and was between flights at the airport. As we were about to board the next plane, I turned my cell phone on and called Debbie in Austin. She asked if I had gotten the message to give her a call. I said no. That's when she told me our beautiful daughter was dead. Around 10:30 that morning, our precious Cammie had taken her own life . . . She went to a small garden area in her backyard, put a large caliber pistol to her chest and pulled the trigger. I fell to my knees screaming that my daughter was dead. Joe Navarro, my employer, who was ahead of me in line, ran back to see what had happened. I was on my knees screaming, "Cammie is dead. My daughter is dead." I was in shock. I was numb. I thought, *This could not be happening, not Cammie.* I can remember feeling like I was going to suffocate. I couldn't breathe. After a while, with Joe's assistance, I was able to somewhat compose myself. Joe arranged with the airlines to get me on the next plane back to Austin. He wanted to come with me, but I insisted that he go ahead and finish the trip.

I got on the next plane home and arrived in Austin around 9:30 p.m. Before boarding the plane for home I called some of our closest friends, Steve and Dedee Norman because Debbie was at home alone. Steve and Dedee immediately went to our house with other close friends, Kevin and Tish McGillicuddy, as well as the Reverend Merrill Wade, the rector of our church, St. Matthew's Episcopal.

When I arrived at the airport in Austin I got disoriented and confused. I could not find my way out of an airport that I had been through dozens of times. I remember sitting and crying for awhile. I felt so devastated, so lost. My baby girl was dead. My precious Cammie was dead. I felt numb. I was in a state of shock. I felt as if my world were coming to an end. In a few minutes I was able to gather enough composure to follow some people out of the airport and to the shuttle to my car.

A police officer and a victim's services advocate representative were just leaving when I arrived home around 10:00 p.m. Somehow things had gotten fouled up and we should have been contacted much earlier in the day about our daughter's death. Unbelievably, our son-in-law did not call us to notify us that Cammie had died.

CHAPTER 12

A DEADLY DECISION

Carmen

"Be merciful to me, O Lord, for I am in distress; my eyes grow
weak with sorrow, my soul and my body with grief."
Psalms 31:9

As Cammie grew up, Larry loved her very deeply and no father could
have enjoyed his child more. Larry was with Cammie in the good
times and he always stood by her through the ups and downs in her
life. Larry truly loved his daughter unconditionally and he became
the kind of father he wanted to be. Larry became the father he would
have liked to have had if his father had lived.

However, Larry and Debbie were inexperienced in dealing with
mental health issues. This inexperience combined with the fact that
Cammie concealed her symptoms, lived in a rural area outside of
Austin, and professed that everything in her life was "fine," made it
very difficult for Larry and Debbie to detect that Cammie's problems
were escalating and her mental health was deteriorating and at a
very rapid pace. By the time Larry and Debbie were informed of
the severity of Cammie's condition, it was already at an emergency
level.

Once Cammie's call came alerting Larry to the severity of her
problems, the fragility of her mental health, and her suicidal ideation,
Larry took swift action to immediately admit her to the local

psychiatric hospital for evaluation and treatment. Even though each case is unique, Larry had no idea how rapidly mental health could deteriorate. He did not understand the complexities of how mental health patients are often released from hospitals in very fragile states and that the psychiatric hospital definition of "stability" is not always clear, accurate, or realistic for fragile patients with emotional pain this intense. Insurance driven mental health all but requires hospitals to release patients, even seriously suicidal patients, much earlier than is truly safe. It is not uncommon for patients to feel overwhelmed by their quick release. Without skills to cope and a support system that is not fully aware of the extreme dangers of quick release, patients continue to use suicide as a primary method to cope. Because a week or two in a mental health facility is often an insufficient amount of time for actively suicidal patients to stabilize, learn new coping skills, and resolve the issues that underlie their ideation, release can be a deadly decision, as was the case with Larry's beloved Cammie.

CHAPTER 13

THE AGONY OF GRIEF

Larry

"Earth has no sorrow that Heaven cannot heal."
Author unknown

Our friends and our rector stayed with Debbie and me for several hours, trying to console us. Just before leaving for the evening my rector, Merrill Wade, took me by the shoulders, got right in my face and told me I was one of the most disciplined men he knew. He also told me it was going to take all of that discipline to get through this. He told me to go lie in the bed beside my wife. He said you won't sleep, but your body will rest, and you have a busy day in front of your tomorrow. He knew that I got up every morning at 5:00 a.m. to work out. So he told me to get up at 5:00 a.m. and exercise. He said I would cry all the way through it, but I needed to maintain the routine. It was part of the discipline.

The next morning started early. After a sleepless night, I got up at 5:00 a.m. and worked out. At 7:00 a.m. I called a dear friend, Fran Moss, and told her what had happened. She was in shock. She couldn't believe what had happened. The next thing we knew she was at our house at 7:30 a.m. Fran just happened to be an organizational genius and we needed her to come and take care of us. God was already sending us help.

This was the longest day of our lives. With Fran's help and guidance, I was able to speak to my son-in-law on the phone. We had not talked to him and I was dreading this conversation, a conversation with the person who abused my child, the person I held at least partially responsible for Cammie's death. Fran sat at my feet and gave me the words to say to him. Debbie and I had resolved that Cammie was going to be buried in Austin not Rockdale. We wanted her close to us. He agreed to let Debbie and I take care of the arrangements and that Cammie could be buried in Austin. When I got off the phone, Debbie looked at Fran and said, "I have just witnessed a miracle!" Fran truly was an angel sent to care for us. I could not have accomplished this on my own. This was Thursday morning, and after many more phone calls and much preparation with our clergy and the funeral home, a celebration of Cammie's life was planned to be held at our church the next Monday afternoon.

It is amazing to me that we were functioning. How does anyone function at a time like this? How do you maintain any composure? How do you even stay on your feet? All you want to do is curl up in a fetal position in bed and cry. Where do you find, not only the strength, but also the energy to do what has to be done at a time like this? No one should ever have to plan their child's funeral, but we had just finished doing that very thing. I still don't know how we did it.

On Saturday afternoon, the family and a few close friends gathered at the funeral home. Judy, Cammie's birth mother, and her stepfather, Rocky, arrived from Montana. On Sunday afternoon, we had a family visitation to receive friends at the funeral home. One thing that I will never forget is seeing the children from Cammie's school. There was one little girl, about seven years old, sitting in the lap of another little girl that was ten or twelve years old. The youngest child could not say anything. She just shook her head and cried. The older girl said she loved Mrs. Springer, that she was her favorite teacher, and that she made learning fun. It was then that I figured out that not only had I lost my daughter, but I had also lost my hero. Cammie helped struggling students learn to read; she helped fearful students learn to add and subtract. She helped students with academic challenges learn to become more confident in their abilities. You see, Cammie didn't just teach reading, writing, and arithmetic, she taught children. She touched their lives. She was so good at what she did.

She loved her children and her children loved her. What a gift she was to them. What a great loss.

I'm a professional salesman. I have been blessed with a great career. I have worked for some of the largest and finest corporations in the world. During my years I have mentored many young people and I know that I have touched and changed lives. I am grateful for that, but Cammie was a teacher. She touched and changed hundreds of lives. Cammie was my hero. She was the apple of my eye. She was her father's daughter.

CHAPTER 14

THIS THING CALLED GRIEF

Carmen

"I can do all things through Christ which strengtheneth me."
Philippians 4:13 KJV

Larry and Debbie knew they had wonderful friends, but had no idea the massive support system that would mobilize to support them through the greatest tragedy of their lives. Larry and Debbie had the biggest hearts and strongest faith of any two people I had known, and their love for others and unwavering faith in God came back to them in ways they never could have imagined.

The advice from Larry's rector to keep up his 5:00 a.m. exercise routine, even through the initial stages of the trauma following Cammie's death, could have sounded extreme to those unfamiliar with healing from unspeakable grief. However, the rector knew that strengthening Larry's mind, spirit, and his body at this time would be critical to his survival. He knew that if Larry could keep up his exercise routine it would continue to strengthen Larry's body through this trauma, and he knew that Larry would need every ounce of strength he could muster to face this trauma.

Larry loved Cammie with all his heart. He was proud of everything she had done. However, until that day at the visitation, he had no idea what a difference Cammie's life had been in the lives of the children with whom she had worked all of her life. When the little girl from Cammie's school told Larry that Cammie had made "learning fun" he suddenly realized the importance of what his little girl had contributed to the world. She had enriched, improved, and touched the lives of hundreds of children with special needs. Larry realized that the life work of Cammie was significant, meaningful, full of purpose, and critically important to the children she had touched. Larry's daughter had made the lives of special needs children a little easier, a little less painful, and had inspired her students to love learning because she made it fun. Cammie had lived a life of service to others in one of the most important ways one human being could help another human being. Although, Cammie had not generated a large income, an important title, or an elevated status in life, the contribution she had made to the betterment of the children of the world was noble and monumental and was reflected in the faces of the children who spoke to Larry that day.

Even though Larry himself, by all standards, had a very successful and lucrative career, had acquired prominence and status in his life, had made deals and money with relative ease, he realized that his success paled in comparison to what his daughter had contributed to the world and to the lives of these innocent children.

Larry and Debbie were experiencing the first stage of grief commonly known as shock and denial. Shock serves an important purpose as it provides a form of temporary insulation from the agonizing pain of the death of a loved one. Larry and Debbie were protected by shock from feeling the full pain of their loss, and this protection allowed them to do the things they had to do to prepare for Cammie's funeral. Larry and Debbie reported experiencing denial periodically in the form of thoughts that would arise in their minds such as, "Surely this is not happening to us," and, "Our precious Cammie cannot be dead." Larry also reported waking up in the morning and feeling a brief absence of awareness that his daughter was dead and then, after those first few moments, feeling the rush of anguish of the reality that his daughter was no longer alive.

CHAPTER 15

A CELEBRATION OF CAMMIE'S LIFE

Larry

"Blessed are those who mourn; for they will be comforted."
Matthew 5:4

Monday, November 19, 2007 was the day we had set to celebrate Cammie's life and lay her earthly body to rest. I asked all the ladies to wear bright colored dresses or dresses with flowers on them. I did not want anyone dressed in black at my daughter's service. This was to be a celebration, a time set aside to celebrate the gift Cammie had been in this world.

I was surprised that the congregation was so large, but Merrill knew it would be and when we planned the service, he asked what priests we would like to participate. Besides Merrill, Susan, and Kevin, the priests at our church, two other friends who were priests came to assist with the service. Mary Wilson did one of the Scripture readings and John Pitts, our former rector, did the homily.

There was a lot I do not remember about the service because I was in so much pain, but I do remember that the sheer number of people in attendance was astonishing to me. What an incredible outpouring of love, an outpouring of love for Cammie and for the entire family. There was a great healing in the service for me because all the pieces had come together so well to honor the daughter I loved so much.

The service was moving. The music was perfect. Jean Farris Fuller, the music director at our church, arranged for a flutist to play at the service. Cammie would have liked that.

After the service at the church we proceeded to the cemetery. Cammie was laid to rest in, as Debbie described, a simply beautiful pine coffin. That would have been Cammie's choice also. After the service was over, Fran ushered Debbie and me to meet a group of teachers from Cammie's school who had come to pay their respects. Fran wanted us to meet them because, unbeknownst to us, about half of the teachers from the school where Cammie taught had come to the visitation at the funeral home on Sunday evening and the other half had come to the funeral on Monday. What an incredible show of love, respect, and admiration from her colleagues. We were deeply touched and overwhelmed by how much Cammie had meant to them.

It seemed that Fran, our guardian angel, had taken care of every detail. She assisted in putting Cammie's service together. She went with us to the funeral home to make all the arrangements for the funeral. She even assisted with the selection of clothing and jewelry for Cammie. Her husband, Steven, a technical writer, even helped me write Cammie's obituary. No one ever wants to plan their child's funeral, but everyone would want that service and everything connected to it, to be perfect, to honor that child. Fran Moss made that possible. What a gift Fran was to us. Everyone should be blessed to have a friend like Fran.

After six days of being incredibly cared for by so many wonderful friends, Debbie and I were finally left alone with our sorrow. At our request, Bob and Glynda Reames, our dear friends from Arlington, had been staying with us for several days. They cared for us. They loved us. They literally helped hold us up during these darkest of days and now they had gone home. The last six days had been an endless outpouring of love from friends and acquaintances. Every meal, everything, and every detail were taken care of. There was not anything that was not seen to. Now there was a void. Now we were alone. We were numb, we were in agony, and we were still in shock. We did not know how to process this type of loss. We kept waiting and thinking that at any moment we would wake up from this dream, this nightmare, and Cammie would still be alive. We did not know where to turn or whom to turn to. Of course, there was our faith, our church, and our incredible friends and family but somehow that still wasn't enough. The pain was too great. We needed some help.

I felt so alone. I was with my precious wife, the love of my life, and I didn't know what to say. I didn't know how to act. I didn't know how to comfort her when my own pain was so great. It was difficult to just maintain my composure. I cried a lot. I cried myself to sleep at night and would wake up, realize Cammie was gone, and start crying again. I was emotionally and physically drained. I was exhausted and did not know where to turn next.

CHAPTER 16

REMEMBERING

Carmen

"He gives strength to the weary and increases
the power of the weak."
Isaiah 40:29

Through the tears, trauma, and brutal pain of the death of Cammie, Larry was somehow able to make many important decisions about the funeral and the service. He wasn't sure how he did it, didn't even remember doing it, but with the help of his devoted friends he and Debbie were able to take action on behalf of Cammie. We are often called on to make some of the most critical decisions any person can make at the most difficult times in our lives, without any experience or preparation to do so.

Eventually, the sweet anesthesia of numbness wore off and Larry and Debbie were left to experience the raw agony of the death of their beloved daughter. They felt the loneliness of their life without the vibrant and vivacious Cammie. They felt the despair of not having the power to change these events in their lives. They were left to try to comprehend that they would have to live in a future without their daughter. They felt the unnatural feelings of being parents who outlive their children. It wasn't supposed to be that way. Parents were supposed to die first, before their children.

It takes great courage to feel and tolerate this type of excruciating pain. It is an act of bravery. It is so agonizing that most people are unable or unwilling to feel these powerful feelings of discomfort. Rather than face up to the ugliness of this type of death, we often, consciously or unconsciously, begin to try to dull the pain through denial, depression, or even drugs and alcohol. It is understandable that the fear of the feeling of going insane from the magnitude of the grief, the feeling of absolute powerlessness, the feeling of total loss of control over the events in our lives can be so overwhelming that we are "driven to drink" or medicate that pain to survive. However, medicating grief can be a trap from which we cannot escape.

We just do the best we can, and Larry and Debbie were no exception. However, there was some type of healthy core within each of them that signaled them to face up to this pain without the temporary anesthesia of alcohol or drugs. They somehow knew they had to face their fears, but how?

Larry and Debbie were in the initial stages of grief commonly known as Shock and Denial and Pain and Guilt. The stages are not discrete and are not necessarily experienced in order. Sometimes the stages are experienced intermittently, sometimes in order and sometimes back and forth. The important thing to know about the stages of grief is that they exist, are a normal and predictable part of the grief process, and are there to help us identify and describe how we are feeling during the bereavement process.

Debbie instinctively knew that getting some significant support and guidance to deal with their pain was needed. She wasn't sure how, but they knew that their wounds were too profound, and the pain exceeded their ability to cope. That instinct to seek help would lead her to pursue the support they needed.

CHAPTER 17

SEARCHING FOR HELP

Larry

"If you're going through hell, keep going."
Winston Churchill

It was the day before Thanksgiving and Debbie and I found ourselves at the cemetery again. As we stood there staring down at Cammie's grave, a stranger came up and startled both Debbie and me. He was a kind, gentle man. He spoke in broken English and in a very soft voice. We finally understood that he was a doctor who lived in El Paso. He was originally from Cuba. He asked what had happened and when we told him the story about Cammie, he said a simple prayer and then informed us that the beautiful lady sitting on a bench about fifty yards from Cammie's gravesite was his wife, sitting at his daughter's gravesite.

His daughter, who was a college student in Austin, had been stalked and murdered three years before. He told me there were still no days without tears. Then he introduced Debbie and me to his wife, and told us about a grief center, a place to seek help after the death of a loved one.

In early December, Fran Moss, the dear friend who had helped Debbie and me with all of Cammie's arrangements and had given us so much support was insistent that I get some professional help. She called Hospice Austin and they had a program that was called,

"Surviving the Holidays." Fran was told that the program would start at 7:00 p.m. at Hyde Park. Debbie, Fran, and I arrived early at Hyde Park Baptist Church on Wednesday evening and, after spending about thirty minutes wandering the cavernous halls, we finally figured out, we either had the wrong night or the wrong location.

The next day, Fran called Hospice and found out that the program had been at Hyde Park Christian Church. There was going to be another program that evening in Dripping Springs. Debbie and I were leaving town on Friday morning and there was no way to make it to the Thursday night meeting. For whatever reason, God kept closing that door. Fran also called the grief center that day and ended up talking to the director who asked Fran to have me call her. This was around noon.

About three o'clock that Thursday afternoon, I was sitting in my car at the cemetery where I found myself going every day. For whatever reason, before getting out of my car, I got on my cell phone and called the grief center and introduced myself, and the receptionist had the director come to the phone. This lady knew exactly how much I was hurting and after we had talked for several minutes, she asked me where I was. I told her I was at the cemetery. She asked me which cemetery and I said Austin Memorial. She said that I was about three blocks from the center and requested that I come by when I left the cemetery. She said that she wanted to give me a hug.

When I left the cemetery, I drove to the grief center. Not only was the director there but her husband was there also. We spent an emotional two hours together. They somehow knew exactly what to say and when to say nothing at all. I left there knowing God had directed me to this place, and I felt hope.

Debbie and I came to the grief center for the first time together in December. One of the staff members who worked at the Center came up and introduced herself to Debbie and me and asked how we found out about the center. Debbie told her that the social worker that came to the house the night Cammie died told her about Hospice Austin and the grief center. Debbie also told her about meeting the man at the cemetery. Upon hearing this story, she turned white as rice. She told us that the man we had met was close friends of the director and that the day after we had met him at the cemetery, he had had a massive stroke and died.

45

CHAPTER 18

A MIRACLE HAPPENED

Carmen

"If you will do what you can do,
God will show up and do what you can't do."
Joel Osteen[1]

Visiting his daughter's grave one week after her death was bittersweet for Larry. He was glad that Cammie was in a beautiful place in the cemetery, but so sad that this was where he had to come to see her now.

It was a lonely time, a raw time, a period when Larry, for the first time in his life, did not know what to do. He had always known what to do before. He had somehow managed to survive the three suicides of his father, uncle, and stepfather, but nothing was like the death of his beloved daughter. Children are not supposed to die before their parents, especially not his vibrant thirty-nine-year-old daughter who appeared to be in the prime of her life. It was too much to bear and so Larry found himself at Cammie's grave daily. Deep inside, Larry wanted to know how to survive the death of Cammie, but had no idea what to do. He had never sought help for this kind of trauma before.

Then a miracle happened, and Larry encountered a man who, unbeknownst to him, was living the last day of his life. And on that last day the man let Larry know about this grief center, a place for bereavement and grief support. Larry's friend, Fran, was strongly encouraging Larry to seek help and support, and on that day, something in Larry led him to risk seeking support from a grief center, a place he had never been to before from people he had not known before, and support was what he got.

The grief center staff all happened to be at the center at just the right time on the right day to meet with Larry. The staff triaged Larry that day as he was in the most acute emotional pain he had ever experienced in his life and needed help from an emotional emergency room. The supportive care Larry got that day gave him just enough hope and enabled him to experience what emotional support felt like. It felt good. It felt like a miracle, like God had allowed Larry to attract just the right help at the just the right time to help him cope with the greatest tragedy of his life. Larry was thankful to God for sending kindness, compassion, and hope that day when he needed it the most.

God truly does work in mysterious ways, and the events that led Larry to the grief center could cynically be viewed as simply a number of coincidences, or could spiritually be viewed as divine guidance. To Larry there was no doubt that it was direct guidance from the divine, from the hand of God.

In the world of recovery, it could be described as Larry "hitting bottom" from the pain of Cammie's death, and as a result, he was now willing to "go to any length" to get the help he needed to heal. Larry asked his Higher Power for help and his Higher Power answered with exactly the help he needed at that time. Somehow I think God knew that if Larry could feel some hope and see a little light at the end of this dark tunnel, he would do whatever it would take to work through this thing called grief.

Larry and Debbie became painfully aware that they were powerless over the death of their child. They employed some twelve-step recovery actions and were able to admit their powerlessness over Cammie's death to one another. This was the first step on their journey to recovery. It took great courage to understand, comprehend, and embrace their powerlessness. Admitting powerlessness is an act of bravery and I knew that their ability to take this step was evidence that they had the strength to do the work of recovery.

Debbie and Larry came to believe that their Higher Power, or God, could lead them to sanity and they made a decision to turn their lives and their wills over to God as they understood him.

CHAPTER 19

GOD SENT HELP

Larry

"Nobody ever told me that grief felt so like fear."
C.S. Lewis[2]

The grief center has a tradition of opening each meeting by passing a stone from one person to another. When you are handed the stone you are supposed to say, "I am here for," and then say that person's name. I am usually never at a loss for words, but that first night at the grief center when the stone was passed to me, I couldn't say anything. All I wanted to do was run out. I handed it to Debbie. For me at that time it was too soon. We went to a small group that night with Carmen Di Nino Alspach for survivors of suicide. There were only three of us in the group.

The big blessing of the evening was being able to share a few of our feelings and meeting Carmen. I called her and scheduled a one-on-one session. Carmen and I have met almost every Thursday night for a one-hour session that usually lasted two hours or longer. I have been doing double time. This is the greatest gift that I have ever given myself. I knew exactly what I was looking for in a counselor. Debbie and I love Carmen and the neat thing is she loves us back. We have formed a special bond.

There are very few things that Carmen does not know about me. We have shared from my youth through Cammie's death. While

I wanted to run out of a large group meeting, I was able to easily and openly share one-on-one with Carmen. I highly recommend individual counseling for anyone that is grieving, especially in the early stages. I think it's easier to share one-on-one, especially early on.

I almost never dream, and if I do, I remember very little if anything about the dream. Sometime in January or February I had a dream. In the dream I was standing in a garage (I think) at the home where my stepfather and mother had lived. Cammie walked into the garage. I looked at her and said, "Darling, you can't be here. You're dead." Cammie came up to me and gave me a hug and told me how much she loved me and she wanted me to know I had done everything that I could do for her. She wanted me to know that she was in a good place. Then I woke up. I could still feel her arms around me. It was as if it had actually just happened and I sat up in bed and cried like a baby.

The road to recovery and restoration is different for each individual. It's the hardest work I've ever done in life. You see, success in life always comes disguised as hard work, and this is no exception. It is hard work. It is physically and emotionally draining. You turn to your faith, family, and your friends to hold you up. I am extremely blessed, I have all three.

CHAPTER 20

HOW TO BEGIN SURVIVING

Carmen

"God is our refuge and strength, an ever-present help in trouble."
Psalms 46:1

If one is fortunate enough to live in a city where a grief center or group is available, it can be a very helpful place to go to for support. Larry had been led to the center in his city and had received the emergency care that gave him that first glimmer of hope. He was told that he could also continue going to the center for ongoing support through attendance at the center's weekly groups. One of the main benefits of going to a support group is that you are able to meet other people who have suffered the death of a beloved person in their lives. Often in our daily lives we do not know others who have survived devastating deaths like we have, and we often feel isolated and alone in our grief.

At grief centers we are able to meet and get to know others like ourselves who are trying to survive the great sadness. Sometimes large groups can be overwhelming for someone new in their grief as was the case with Larry. Larry and Debbie felt more comfortable in the small group for the family members of loved ones who completed their deaths by suicide.

However, sometimes one's pain is so great that working individually with a therapist familiar with grief, especially grief from loss of a loved one by suicide, can be a more effective place to start. Larry told me that he felt comfortable working with me in the group and would like to begin individual counseling sessions as soon as possible. Larry knew that, although he had many skills, great strength and deep faith, he had no idea how to begin surviving and dealing with the death of his beloved daughter.

Later, I was to learn that this was not the first suicide Larry had had to bear. He had also experienced the suicides of his father, stepfather, and uncle years before Cammie's death. Four deaths by suicide in a single family was highly unusual and the toll on Larry's life could only be imagined.

Little was Larry to know that he had chosen a therapist uniquely qualified in the areas of grief, death by suicide, and family systems therapy. So the man attempting to survive four family deaths by suicide and the therapist well acquainted with grief and suicidal ideation began their work together. Sometimes people would ask me how my clients were referred to me and I would reply that God sends them to me. God allows me to help him with their healing. The whole series of events that led Larry to my office did indeed seem like divine intervention.

Now, typically, therapists see their clients for one hour per week. But having the advantage of coming from a diverse background of counseling styles and experiences, I allowed myself the freedom to individually adapt the type of counseling and format best suited to each person. Larry was definitely one of the hardest working clients I had ever seen. Once he understood that healing was possible and that there was a light in the darkness, he wanted to work as hard as he could for as long as it took to heal. He knew Cammie would not want her death to have led to the downfall of her father, and if there was a way to survive and heal from her death, Larry was willing to do that work and work as hard as he could.

Therapists can often determine the motivation of their clients by asking two simple questions: "Have you had enough (pain)?" and, "Are you willing to go to any length to heal?" Larry responded a resounding "yes" to both of these questions. I knew this was an excellent predictor for a positive prognosis for Larry.

Larry had a couple of questions for me. "How does therapy work," and, "How will I know when it is over?" I told him that he would come in regularly for weekly sessions and we would explore every aspect of his losses together and that he would be completely in control of the pacing of the therapy. We would go as fast or slow as was comfortable for him. I told him that he would be learning many tools and strategies that would help him in his recovery and that he would absolutely know when therapy was over because he would feel much better and stronger and would come in one day and say, "I think I am done!"

When Larry began his therapy he worked harder than any client I had ever worked with. His desire to heal was very clear and very strong to me. He came to a one—or two-hour session per week for about a year and a half and made significant progress at each session. I was fully confident that healing would come to Larry.

Although therapy can be painful because of the sensitive and raw feelings and issues that must be confronted and resolved, it also provides significant relief once the restoration begins. Larry felt that pain and also some of that relief and said that the therapy felt good to him and gave him hope for the future.

A favorite picture of Cammie

Larry, Debbie, Cammie and Tiffany

Simons Family Christmas 1954

PART TWO

JOURNEY

to

WHOLENESS

THE TOOLS

CHAPTER 21

LIVING IN GRIEF

Larry

"You don't heal from the loss of a loved one because time passes;
you heal because of what you do with the time."
Carol Staudacher[3]

In the first part of this book I have told you the story of my life and about the tragedies in my life. The loss of my father, my uncle, and my stepfather all had huge impacts on my life, but nothing compared to the death of my precious daughter. Cammie's death brought me to my knees. It stopped and changed my entire world. I wanted the world to stop so I could get off.

How do you handle this kind of grief? I was numb. I was in shock. My heart was broken. I had dealt with major losses in my life before, but nothing compared to this. How did I get from November 14, 2007 to March 1, 2009, a sixteen-month period of time, and go from the greatest sadness of my life to back to being excited about life again? How was it possible?

I went through what most people would refer to as the traditional stages of grief, the whys, the what if's, the pain, the sorrow, the anguish, the anger, the trying to understand why my beautiful daughter could take her own life. I went through the temporary insanity, the memory loss, a body in constant state of dis-ease. Couldn't sleep, couldn't think, and couldn't function. My life was lived in a daze. I kept wanting to wake up from this dream, this nightmare. It would happen to me several times a day. I would close my eyes and think this has to be a dream. Nothing can be this bad, nothing can hurt this bad. I just knew that when I opened my eyes, I would wake up from the nightmare, but it didn't happen! It wasn't a dream; the nightmare continued.

I needed to try to understand this thing called suicide, this thing that keeps occurring in my life, in my family. What is this thing that keeps taking away people I love? What is this thing that has brought me to my knees, that has brought me to the bottom?

I had heard people talk about "hitting bottom." For me the bottom was dark, lonely, scary, frightening. I questioned everything in life. I questioned my religion, my faith, my sanity. For the first time in my life, I was having difficulty coping with day-to-day life. I could not function. I was constantly sick. I felt fragile. I was fragile. Would I break? Would this pain ever end or would my life be like this forever?

Thank heaven for an incredible wife and friends who saw the depth of my pain and knew I needed help to survive. As much as they loved me, they knew I needed more than just their love. They could not love me out of this. This was a time for professional help. I was losing the battle on my own. I needed help and I needed it now. Thank heaven for the grief center. Thank heaven for the incredible Carmen, my counselor, my "new best friend" who spent untold hours helping me see that there was light at the end of the tunnel. Thank heaven for thirty plus years of studying what makes people tick. Thank heaven for my tools. I was to learn that the tools that I had used to be successful in business and build a successful life could also be used to help me recover from this incredible grief.

Living in grief is not living. How do you, how did I, recover? In the next few chapters of this book I will share with you my journey, my journey from incredible grief, from a life that was not functioning, back to wholeness. This is what I call the journey to wholeness.

I had sought help many times in business. I have spent thousands of hours studying the lives of successful people and what made them successful. I had never sought help for my own mental health, but I knew that oftentimes successful people do just that—they seek guidance, they seek help. Now was the time for me to seek help.

I am a great believer in the law of attraction. I attracted everything and everyone I needed into my life. I knew exactly the kind of person I was looking for in a counselor even though I had never done this before. I was very clear to Debbie that if I were to go into counseling, the counselor had to be a woman. I knew I was looking for guidance. I knew I was looking for answers. I knew it would feel right with the right person. I wanted to be able to be open and honest and share my deepest pain. I found that person.

After meeting Carmen at the grief center about a month after Cammie's death, I thought I had found the right person. I had at least found a person I was willing to try to talk to. This was new to me. This was new territory where I wasn't in control. I am used to being in control. I like being in control! I wanted to know how it worked. What would we talk about, how long would it take? How would I know if I was getting better, how would I know when it is over?

Seeking help of this type is something I never thought I would do or need. I needed help and, after our first session, I knew I had attracted the right person into my life at just the right time. If I felt uncomfortable, I could always quit, but talking to Carmen was comfortable. I felt I could be open, honest, and share my pain, my wounded soul. Our time together gave me an opportunity to share openly and honestly all the pains of my life.

Counseling gave me new hope. I had hit bottom. I have always functioned at a very high level and now I was barely able to function at all. Life hurt. It hurt to be alive. It hurt to live. I didn't care and I usually cared a lot. Counseling gave me a new promise, a promise of recovery and a lot more.

This was the hardest work I had ever done in my life. I had to be brutally honest about all of my feelings. I had to feel all of my feelings and it hurt! It hurt a lot. There were lots of tears. I don't remember much of our first few sessions, but I don't remember much about the first few weeks and months following Cammie's death either. I was alive, but not really living. After a while, I began to look forward to my counseling sessions. Debbie looked forward to my counseling sessions and would suggest topics, questions, and things to discuss. She supported me and urged me to go.

After each counseling session I would go home and discuss the entire session with Debbie. Our Thursday nights were always very late. My one-hour sessions with Carmen never lasted one hour. Most sessions were two hours long. Carmen said I was doing double time. She noticed how hard I was working. As I said before, this is hard work. There was nothing easy about bearing my soul to another person. This was probably the most honest I had ever been with myself in life and to my surprise, it felt good.

All of this was very enlightening to me. I found out a great deal about myself. I dealt with many old wounds, the suicides of my father, my stepfather, and my uncle. Wounds I had had for many years, wounds that had never healed. I had not realized the impact the trauma of these deaths had had on my life. Now, with Cammie's death, it felt like someone had ripped my heart right out of my body. My incredibly beautiful and talented daughter was dead. The nightmare was never going to end. I would never have her back. I had to find a way to live with the pain.

These sessions were about healing, the healing of my mind, my body, and my spirit. Plato said that there would be no healing until a person is treated mind, body, and spirit.

Within the first few months of counseling, several things became very clear to me. I now had a goal. How does one have a goal in grief? I know that may sound odd, but for me, there was a goal, a goal to move through the grief back to wholeness. It was about not getting stuck in grief because that would have been all about me. It was about finding a way to honor Cammie. To honor her life and the contributions she made. Her life made the world a better place and that was what I wanted to remember the most. I told Carmen I wanted to find a way to honor Cammie. Carmen said that together we would find a way, and when we did, it would be big.

CHAPTER 22

NOT GETTING STUCK

Carmen

"The Lord is close to the brokenhearted and
saves those who are crushed in spirit."
Psalm 34:18 NIV

Larry's story is unique in that it is highly unusual for an individual to experience so many deaths by suicide in a single family. Although suicidal ideation is not genetically passed on through generations, the use of suicide as a coping mechanism can be passed on behaviorally. Even having a single death by suicide in a family tacitly lets family members know that suicide is a legitimate option in that family. No one says it out loud, but the more fragile or highly stressed family members learn from modeling that this coping mechanism can be considered as an option for coping.

Larry and Cammie had three family members model that suicide is a viable option to cope. Larry did not acquire a suicidal ideation because he had so many other strong and successful coping mechanisms in his arsenal. Cammie did not appear to use suicide as a coping mechanism in her earlier life, not until life got so agonizingly painful and hopeless that she saw it as the only way she could get relief from her pain.

We do not know whether a suicidal ideation would ever have been developed as a coping mechanism by Larry following the death of Cammie. The pain was certainly excruciating enough to trigger an ideation in even the strongest of people. There was a very real possibility it could have been acquired, but Larry sought help so quickly following Cammie's death, and he learned such a wide array of ways to cope that he never had to feel trapped, hopeless, and desperate enough to consider suicide as an option.

The divine guidance continued for Larry and he attracted the right group with the right counselor at precisely the right time to get the help he needed. Even though he had never worked with a therapist before and wasn't sure how it even worked, he was in enough pain to risk reaching out for this type of help.

Therapists have kind of an unspoken guideline with their clients that the therapist does not work harder than the client. This guideline is to help therapists prevent enabling their clients. From the first minutes of that first session I quickly saw what all therapists want to see in their clients—the strong desire to heal. Larry said that, indeed, he was willing to go to any length to heal. He was willing to do the work even if it meant feeling the dreaded feelings of grief that hurt so badly. Larry seemed to instinctively know that there was not enough medication, not enough alcohol, not enough drugs in the world to prevent him from feeling this pain. He knew it was pay now or pay later. He knew he must face this grief, but that he did not have to face it alone. God sent guidance in the form of a therapist who could help him walk through the terrible minefields of acute, complicated grief and into healing and restoration.

Instinctively Larry was led to choose me to be his guide. It has been a privilege. Larry asked me where my clientele came from and I told him that God sends them to me. I have no doubt that God sent Larry to my office, gave him the strength to make that first call, and would be with him on his journey into wholeness and restoration. Before every session with my clients I say a little prayer and ask God to come into the session with me and to use me as a tool to do his will. I truly believe in my spirit and in my soul that God used me as a tool to help Larry heal. As we will see further along on his journey, God had some plans to use Larry as a tool to do his will as well.

Larry was one of the most hardworking clients I have ever worked with. Larry was able to adopt some key strategies to being able to successfully live with grief. Larry was able to ask for help. He was able to be honest about his feelings. He had the courage to talk about his feelings and was willing to feel the excruciating pain of grief without medicating himself with alcohol or drugs. And Larry was able to make the choice to focus his thoughts primarily on the blessing of having thirty-nine years with his beloved Cammie rather than primarily focusing on her death.

In grief we always have that choice to stay stuck in thinking about the death of our loved ones or to shift our focus on the joy of their lives. Some people even feel guilty about focusing on the joy of the loved one's life and when asked, will often say that focusing on the loved one's life rather than the death feels disrespectful, because of the false impression that the longer we hold on to the grief the more love we have for the loved one. However, we now know that the reverse is true. We now know that focusing on the death is all about us and our pain while focusing on the loved one's life is all about the loved one. Larry indicated that he wanted to focus on the gratitude he had for God for granting him thirty-nine years with Cammie prior to her death.

CHAPTER 23

CHOOSING YOUR ATTITUDE

Larry

"Anything the mind can conceive and believe it can achieve."
Napoleon Hill[4]

When Cammie died, I felt broken. I **was** broken. To fix anything that is broken, you need tools. For me, the most important tool in life has always been to maintain a good attitude. The first tool I realized I was using was simply having a good attitude. Attitude is the base which all of the other tools depend upon. I had every reason in the world to have a lousy attitude. I felt I had a right to one. Others even expected me to, but I understood through my studies the importance of having a good or right attitude. I learned as a teenager from a very wonderful mentor and coach, Coach Roger Wilke. Coach taught me that winning and losing on the football field was ten percent know-how and ninety percent attitude and that most things in life worked the same way. Life truly is ten percent know-how and ninety percent attitude. Coach Wilke had a lasting influence on my life, on my attitude. Coach Wilke was a great gift.

The greatest discovery of my generation is that human beings can alter their lives by altering one thing—their attitudes of mind. I think that bears repeating, the greatest discovery of my generation is that human beings can alter their lives by altering one thing—their attitudes of mind. I wish I could take credit for saying that for the first time, but William James, back around 1894 or 1895, spoke those words originally. William James is the father of modern psychology.

How do you have a good attitude in the midst of grief and pain? How do you put it all together when it seems like your whole world has collapsed around you? There are all kinds of grief. My great grief was the death of my daughter by suicide. It brought me to my knees. It brought me to a new bottom in life that I had never been to before.

There are all kinds of grief in the world, especially in today's society with the loss of income, the loss of savings, the loss of jobs, divorce, broken families, and war. There is so much grief in the world. This grief brings on new grief because the suicide rate is at an all-time high.

How do we in life have a good attitude in the midst of all this pain? I want to give you some ideas to use that have helped me in my life to be successful in business and in life. Now these same tools have helped me work through this incredible grief. Notice I said *work through*, not around, not over, not under, but work through the grief.

How do you have a good attitude? Where does it start? It starts with a decision. You decide to have a good attitude. When people ask me today how I am doing, I tell them I am wonderful. It is hard to say *I'm wonderful* and kick the dog at the same time. People look at me like I am strange, or weird, or maybe even crazy. How can I be wonderful when they know what has gone on in my life? They know what I have been going through after the death of my daughter. How can I be wonderful? It is a decision. It is a decision I make every day when I get out of bed.

When my feet hit the floor in the morning, I start saying thank you. I take my little dog Sophie outside and on the way out I say, "Thank you, God, for Sophie." Sophie's love for me is unconditional, just like God's love for me. I say, "Thank you, God, for Debbie. Thank you, God, for Cammie. Thank you, God, for Dawn. Thank you, God, for my grandchildren. Thank you, God, for Carmen. Thank you, God, for all of our incredible extended family." I start thanking God for everything in my life. I don't just say thank you, I keep saying thank you, until the hair on the back of my neck stands up and I feel the thanks. I truly feel the thanks in my life. I feel the gratitude. It is an incredible way to start the day.

How did I get there? The first thing is that I had a great understanding of what attitude is and I don't think most people do. Now let me explain this. We are told as small children that if we change our attitudes, that things are going to go better for us. We are told by our teachers in school that if we change our attitudes, our grades will improve. We are told by our coaches that if we change our attitudes, our performance will greatly improve. We are told as sales people that if we change our attitudes, our sales will increase. Marriage counselors tell married couples that if they will change their attitudes, their marriages will improve. We are taught throughout life that if we change one thing, our attitudes, everything in life will improve. It is the same way in grief recovery—if we change our attitudes, everything does get better.

Ask the next person you meet to give you the definition of the word *attitude*. Chances are they can't give it to you. You would think that anything as important as this word attitude would be known by everyone; the sad thing is that it is known by a very few.

I want to attempt to give you what I think is the best definition of attitude that I have ever heard in life. But first let me explain how I think God put us together. We have three parts to us. We have our conscious mind, our educated mind, the part of us that thinks. We have our subconscious mind, the spiritual or emotional part of our personality, and it's the part of us that feels. And then we have our physical body, the part that acts out our thoughts and feelings.

In today's world it is called the cognitive behavioral process. Our thoughts (T) cause our feelings (F) which cause our actions (A). T $\rightarrow$ F $\rightarrow$ A. Understanding this concept in grief is critical. Understanding this concept will make THE difference between healing and wholeness or being eternally stuck in grief.

Let me explain the three parts of this concept to you. T = the thinking mind or the part that thinks. But before I go any further, I do not want you to mistake the *mind* for the brain. No one really knows what mind is. Mind is not a thing, it is an activity. Within our thinking mind we have the ability to think (T); that is what separates us from all of the other animals in the world. We can choose our thoughts. We can reason. The Bible says that we are given "dominion over." We can think. We can choose what we think—our thoughts.

One must come to an understanding that *thoughts are things*. So in the midst of our incredible grief, we have to recognize what we are thinking about. Therefore we get to choose our thoughts about our loss, about our grief. Then we send these thoughts to our feeling minds (F), the part of us that feels.

The feeling mind (F) differs from the thinking mind in that it cannot reject any thought. All thought that is fed into the feeling mind is accepted, good or bad, positive or negative. The feeling mind says one thing to every thought that enters. It says YES. For example, choosing the thought, "This death, this loss, is destroying me," and feeding this thought into our feeling mind over and over again, will cause us to feel sad and frightened. It will cause us to act negatively. It will immobilize us. We must remember the feeling mind always says YES even if the thoughts are negative.

The acting out, the action (A) is done by the body. The body is simply the servant to the mind. The body carries out all the thoughts and feelings of the mind.

Happy thoughts are hopeful thoughts such as, "Thank you, God, for my daughter, Cammie"; "Thank you, God, for loaning this precious spirit to me for thirty-nine years!" Remembering I never owned her. She was just on loan from God. These thoughts caused me to feel thankful, to feel happy, and to have an attitude of gratitude. These thoughts caused me to act positively, to energize me, to strengthen me to make it through the day. The feeling part of the mind says YES to positive or happy thoughts.

How in the midst of incredible grief can one decide to have happy or hopeful thoughts? One can CHOOSE to. It is not easy. You make a conscious decision. You choose your thoughts every single day. You choose not to get stuck in grief. You choose to have an attitude of gratitude rather than an attitude of self-pity.

Any thought that YOU choose to think over and over again leads you to feel the way you feel. It leads you to feel the way you think, positively or negatively, good or bad. The very best definition I have ever heard of attitude is simply this:

Attitude is our mental position or state of mind expressed by our thoughts, feelings, and actions. T → F → A

Where are you now in life? What are you thinking, feeling, and doing? There are three parts to us, our THINKING mind, our FEELING mind, and our ACTIONS. You choose your thoughts, you feed them into your FEELING mind, and the thoughts cause you to feel the way you feel and then lead you to act the way you act.

We are NOT in control of what has happened to us, but we ARE in control of how we choose to THINK. We are in control of choosing our thoughts. Choosing hopeful thoughts will cause us to feel optimistic, and cause our actions to be positive.

It is critically important to know this in our healing process. It is vitally important to know this in life. It was important for me to know this in my career, but even more vital to know this in my grief. My life DEPENDED on it. It was that important.

Thoughts are everywhere about us. How do we go about choosing good thoughts? How do we know when we are having negative thoughts? There is this thing that we do all of the time called "self-talk." We are in a constant dialogue with ourselves all day long. We have between fifty and sixty thousand thoughts a day! The idea of choosing which ones are positive and which ones are negative seems like an impossible job, but you know it is not.

Do you know how to determine how you are having a negative or destructive thought? It is simple. A negative or destructive thought causes you to feel bad. It causes you to feel negative. So, if you are feeling negative or are feeling down, then the thing to do is to stop and choose to think an uplifting or more positive thought even if you don't exactly feel like it at the time.

In the depths of grief, this is not easy. It is not easy a lot of times in life, but remember, success in life always comes disguised as hard work. This is hard work! This is the hardest work I have ever had to do in my life! It is the hardest work you will ever have to do in your life! To make it through the grief back to wholeness takes a lot of hard work. You have to choose to do this. It is your decision. You can choose the positive or happy thoughts, and send those thoughts to that God-like part of you, your FEELING mind, which will then lead you to feel hopeful and act the same way. Any thoughts that are fed into the FEELING mind over and over again will cause you to feel and act accordingly. Positive or negative—the choice is yours even in grief.

I am not saying that choosing positive thoughts is easy, especially at this point in your life. I am a lifelong student of this type of thinking and it was still difficult for me. There were many days when it was hard just to get out of bed and function. There were days when choosing optimistic thoughts seemed impossible, but I knew I had a choice and I knew it was my choice, a choice to heal, a choice of returning to wholeness or a choice of being stuck in eternal grief. Given that choice, I choose life.

That is why it is so important to understand the definition of attitude and the importance it plays in your life, the importance it plays in your recovery. Attitude is made up of thoughts, feelings, and actions. The attitude you choose to have could be the *single most important tool* in determining how and when you recover. It will determine *if* you recover.

There are several things I do each day to maintain a constructive or positive attitude and it has helped so much in my recovery. I continue to set aside time each day to work on the three parts of my personality—mind, body and spirit. I continue to get up at 5:00 each morning for my exercise routine. The exercise is great for the body, and it's a great stress reliever, so that's good for the mind and the spirit. I read while I'm on the elliptical. This helps me feed my mind and my spirit. I also set aside a time for prayer each day. All of this affects my attitude. It helps me maintain an encouraging or positive attitude.

Over the last thirty plus years, I have read books that have changed and helped direct my life. Each of the authors understood how God put us together. The first few books I read after Cammie died were books about grief and the grieving process. After reading several books on grief that were very good, I came to a better understanding of the grief process. But I needed something different, I needed some comfort food, I needed something to feed my mind and my spirit. I found the comfort food that I needed, with some old and new friends. These authors understood that thoughts are things and the importance of an optimistic attitude. A suggested reading list of my favorite authors and titles are listed at the end of this book. These books are incredible tools. I feel each one is a "hand of God" book. I feel God's hand was on the authors hand when the books were being written. My books have played a very important role in my recovery.

Attitude truly is everything. The ninety-ten rule always holds true for me. Life is ten percent know-how and ninety percent attitude! In the depths of my grief, I found I could stop thinking how terrible it was that Cammie died. Cammie led an incredible life. Cammie's life touched and changed the lives of so many people, people I will never know. She touched the lives of students, faculty, friends, and family through the way she lived her life and through the occupation she chose, being a special education teacher.

When Cammie walked into a room, she filled the room with sunshine. Some people have that ability because of their positive attitude about life. Cammie's life was an incredible example for me. I get to choose the thoughts of how I remember my daughter. I get to remember how she touched and influenced so many hearts and lives with her incredible love. By choosing thoughts like these about Cammie, my attitude can only be positive.

It is a great tragedy that Cammie is not with me, but it is a great gift to have been her father for thirty-nine years! She was a great gift to the whole world. This is what I have an opportunity to concentrate on. This is what I have to think about, the gift. This is choosing a happy thought and sending that thought over and over again to my FEELING mind which causes me to feel good. It causes me to feel wonderful! It causes me to act in the same manner.

Attitude is our mental position or state of mind expressed by our thoughts, feelings, and actions. Where are you right now? If you are not where you want to be, you can change it by changing one thing, changing your thoughts. Thoughts truly are things. Changing your thought patterns changes your entire outlook or attitude on life. It is the beginning point of success. It is the beginning point of recovery. For me, everything changed when I began to THINK primarily about the LIFE of my precious Cammie and her contribution to the world, rather than thinking primarily about her untimely death.

Please don't get stuck in grief. Please think about what you are thinking about. Everything good starts with a positive or happy attitude, especially in grief. Always remember THOUGHTS (T) cause FEELINGS (F) which then cause ACTIONS (A).

Attitude is our mental position or state of mind expressed by our thoughts, feelings and actions. T → F → A

CHAPTER 24

YOU HAVE A CHOICE

Carmen

"You are, and you become, what you think about."
Earl Nightingale

On the surface, even thinking about having a good or positive attitude in the middle of profound grief sounds impossible or even crazy. The grief response following a tragic or traumatic death can be monumental. Just surviving following the death can take every ounce of energy one has and Larry experienced this response in the weeks following Cammie's death. However, once Larry got into therapy and began to see that first glimpse of hope, the relief gave him just enough energy to consider the attitude he wanted to have regarding his recovery.

The first time I noticed Larry's remarkable attitude was when I began to see the enthusiasm he had for doing the work required in therapy. Psychotherapy is similar to physical therapy in that it is a process, which is often painful, but through exercising and practicing new behaviors, improving and strengthening physical or emotional responses, a person's life begins to gradually improve. Even though Larry knew the therapy would be painful, he chose to have a positive attitude about his therapy because he thought it would eventually help him to heal, to feel better, and to regain wholeness.

Larry could have chosen to have a negative attitude about his therapy, but he knew it would make the therapy process even more painful if he thought about it negatively. Now, I asked him how he was able to have such a positive attitude in his grief and he said that any process of restoration that he believed would help him to heal his broken heart, regain his sanity, and place him on a journey to wholeness was a process about which he could genuinely feel positive.

Larry knew that having a positive attitude about anything important in life would always be helpful and having a negative attitude would always make things more difficult if not impossible. This philosophy made sense to him and had worked for him for many years in his private and professional life. But this philosophy had worked during times of low and moderate stress, and Larry had to think about whether it would work during this time of the highest stress and greatest emotional pain he had ever felt in his life. He had to think about whether he could realistically have a positive attitude when he was hurting so badly.

Larry told me that having a positive attitude was a decision a person makes and did not have to be dependent upon his feelings. He knew that he could choose to think positively whether he was feeling good or feeling bad. Feeling good was not a prerequisite. In fact, if he wanted to begin feeling better, having a positive attitude would be an essential requirement. He also knew he could use the "fake it 'til you make it" strategy until he could genuinely have a positive attitude about his recovery. My observation let me know that it was only a short time into the therapy before Larry would move from the "fake it" mode into having a genuinely positive attitude.

We know that self-talk in grief is very important, because what we think about the death leads directly to the feelings we feel about our loss. If we think about the death as a catastrophe, the end of the world, we will feel hopeless, victimized, and depressed. Whereas, if our self-talk is about the gift of the loved one in our lives, the more hopeful we will feel about the gift rather than the loss. Choosing to primarily think about the death rather than primarily about the life is all about us and our pain, whereas thinking about the gift of the loved ones in our lives is all about honoring our loved ones.

CHAPTER 25

THERE IS A GOAL IN GRIEF

Larry

"Start by doing what's necessary; then do what's possible; and
suddenly you are doing the impossible."
St. Francis of Assisi

I am a very goal-oriented person. By this I mean I have a long
standing habit of setting long and short range goals. I was taught
how to do this by the masters. I know the importance it has played in
my life. I have used this tool to set and attain personal and business
goals. I have used this tool to attain both physical and spiritual or
emotional goals, but what does goal setting have to do with grief
recovery? I think a lot.

Several months after Cammie's death and several months into
counseling my old habits started to kick in. I was thinking more
clearly. I was thinking that I had to find a way out of this incredible
grief. I knew that this grief could destroy my life if I let it.

People form habits and habits form lives. I have formed habits
that have helped me be successful in life and now these same habits
were starting to work for me in grief recovery.

My habit of goal setting kicked in and I started to think that there
had to be a better way to live. I started to understand what this thing
called grief was doing to my life. I started to understand the toll grief
was having on my life.

My main goal in life became working through the grief back to wholeness. There is a lot to this goal. I knew it would be a hard journey and a great deal of hard work, but I also understood it could save my life. I could not, would not let this grief destroy me.

What role do goals play? What is their importance? Let me explain how and why I think goal setting is important in life, how and why I go about goal setting, and the importance it had in my recovery, and the importance it can have on your life and in your recovery.

Harry Emerson Fosdick, a great theologian, said, "For any life to be great it has to be focused, dedicated, and disciplined." I want to review what Fosdick said. *For any life to be great it has to be focused.* We must have ideas, goals we are striving for. We have to know exactly where we are going. *For any life to be great it has to be dedicated.* We must have a burning desire; we must fall in love with our goals, our ideas. *For any life to be great it has to be disciplined.* We must discipline ourselves to do the hard work, to do whatever it takes to reach our goals. This is great advice for life. This is a must in grief recovery.

I was *focused.* I had a goal. I was striving for healing. I was *dedicated*; I had a burning desire. I wanted my life to be restored to wholeness. I was *disciplined*; I did the work, the hard work it takes in recovery. I did not run away from the pain.

I believe we can reach any goal that we can see, that we can visualize. If we can see ourselves, visualize ourselves, hold the picture in our minds of ourselves reaching our goals, we have it within our power to reach whatever goals, whatever destinations we choose.

The great Napoleon Hill said, "Anything the mind can conceive and believe it can achieve."

You may ask what the purpose of a goal is. Why do I need to set a goal? The only purpose, the only real importance of a goal is to assist in our growth. We have been taught by both science and theology that there is a great power within us. We are taught that we can bring that power to bear, to achieve anything we truly want to achieve. I wanted healing and wholeness more than anything in life. I knew I needed to make healing my ultimate goal. I knew if I did that, I could be successful.

Success is a word that is misunderstood by most people. I think success can be best defined as the progressive realization of a worthy idea. Our goals are important, but we must always remember that goals are the destination. Success is the journey. This means that we have begun to be successful on our journey to wholeness the moment we decide what our goals are and start to move in the direction of our goals. That is success one day, one step at a time.

We must desire healing. Our desire for healing must become a white hot flame. Desire is the driving force that moves us in the direction of our goals. Philosopher and author, Wallace D. Waddles, said, "Desire is the effort of an unexpressed possibility within, seeking expression without, through our actions."

We must be able to visualize ourselves reaching our goals. We must be able to see what our lives will look like, feel like once we reach the goal of recovery. This will start moving us in the direction of our goals.

Solomon, who lived ten centuries before Christ and was one of the wealthiest and wisest people to ever live, said that where there is no vision, the people will perish. We must have goals. They are our road map, pointing us in the right direction. In life we are either moving ahead or we are moving backward. In recovery, we must make a decision to move ahead. It is a choice. It is our choice. We must have a goal. Remember what Solomon said, "Where there is no vision [no goal], the people will perish."

We need to write our goals down on paper. Writing creates thinking. I have my goal written on a card that I carry in my pocket. I have done this for many years. I have never failed to reach a goal that I have written down and carried with me. Every time I reach in my pocket and touch that card the picture of my goal flashes on the screen of my mind. It is positive thoughts that move me in the direction of my goal. It is positive thoughts that move me toward healing, toward recovery.

I love what James Allan wrote in his wonderful book, *As a Man Thinketh*. He wrote "As you think you travel. As you love you attract. You will realize the vision not the idle wish." See, we cannot just wish for our goals' achievement. We have to know in our hearts that we can reach them. The problem is that most people wish positively and think negatively.

There will be days when the plan just doesn't work, days when we will hit plateaus. Plateaus are to be expected. The law of rhythm, which we will discuss in the next chapter, says that nothing is always up and nothing is always down. There are going to be days when you are not at your peak, days when you just feel down. Realize this and do not let it deter you. You must still hold the picture of your goal of healing in your mind. It is not going to be easy. It will be tough, but it can be done.

The next thing you need to do is break your goal into small parts. It may be difficult to see all the steps you need to take when you can barely make it through the day. You might try to break your day into small parts so it is not so overwhelming. Try breaking your day down into three parts, the time until lunch, the time until dinner, and the time until you go to bed. In the morning when you get up, put everything you've got into the morning. Anyone can do anything from breakfast until lunch. At lunchtime give it all you have until dinner and after dinner give it all you have until you go to bed. If you will do this and continue to visualize and hold the picture of healing and wholeness in your mind, and remember why you are doing this, you will be moving in the direction of your goal. You will be moving in the direction of wholeness and healing.

As I stated earlier, the only purpose of a goal is the growth, the healing that we experience as we work toward it. Success is the journey. Success is achieved one step, one day at a time. Reaching the goal is important, but the growth, the true success in life is in the journey, and no one can ever take that kind of true success from you.

I want to give you a passage from one of my heroes in life, Theodore Roosevelt. He said, "Far greater it is to have done mighty things, to win glorious triumphs, even though checkered by failure, than to take ranks with those poor spirits who live in that grey twilight that knows not victory nor defeat."

You may fall down a thousand times. I did. You have to get up a thousand and one times.

I want you to think about this—you have an enormous power within you that will give you anything you truly want, including healing and restoration. You can reach any goal that you can visualize. You can be restored to wholeness.

CHAPTER 26

THE JOURNEY

Carmen

"Dreams are the seedlings of realities."
James Allen

A tool that had brought Larry great professional success and a lucrative income was a tool called goal setting. Larry had used the tool of goal setting every day for the previous twenty-five or thirty years. He had set goals and achieved them over and over and over again in business with great success. He even utilized a tool called a "goal card." He would write his goal on his goal card and keep it in his pocket every day until that goal was accomplished and then set another goal to achieve. I asked him how he was using that tool in his recovery and he said that he was using it by setting a specific goal for his grief recovery. He said that he wanted to have a goal in grief so he would know whether he was making progress or not. Larry had observed some people who looked like they were "stuck" in some kind of eternal grief. He knew that if he got stuck in the hell of eternally feeling grief and sorrow he would not make it. Larry knew that he would always miss his beloved Cammie, but that he wanted to heal and move through the trauma of her death and into the light of glorious gratitude. Larry knew that Cammie would want this for him as well.

I asked Larry to tell me about the goal he had for his grief recovery. He said that he had a very specific goal to "move through the grief and into wholeness." He wanted to be happy again. He wanted to feel better. He wanted to go from focusing on the death of Cammie and his own personal sorrow to focusing on the fact that Cammie had been a beautiful gift to him from God. Larry had been given the honor and privilege of having Cammie on loan to him here on earth for thirty-nine years and he wanted to focus on the tremendous gratitude he felt for the magnificent gift of being her father for all of those years.

As I watched the amazing transformation of Larry from a man of sorrow who had been broken and battered by the tragic death of Cammie into a humble, healing, and monumentally thankful man, I felt great joy for the privilege of watching the miracle. He became a man who was fully aware that he could easily not have had this precious gift at all and that it was only by the grace of God that he had been chosen to be her father. He became a man overflowing with gratitude and appreciation for the gift he had been given. He became a man who was reaching his goal of being on a journey toward wholeness.

Larry was gradually healing, recovering, and becoming whole again and it felt good! By keeping his mind focused on his goal of healing and recovery, he went from being a man focused on himself and his sorrow and the great pain he was feeling into a man who was now focused on gratitude for the life of Cammie and for all of the good that she had contributed to the world. Larry said that it felt good to go from thinking about himself and his pain and tragedy twenty-four hours a day to thinking about Cammie and the gifts she had given to him and to others twenty-four hours a day.

When Larry thought about his goal of healing and returning to wholeness he automatically felt hopeful, he had direction and meaning in his life. Once his goal had been established Larry said he began to feel better. Every time he thought about his goal he felt better. Every time he took a step toward his goal he felt better. Every time he realized that his goal could be attained through diligent, consistent grief work he felt better.

CHAPTER 27

HEALING THE MIND: UNDERSTAND NATURAL LAW

Larry

"Shallow men believe in luck,
wise and powerful men, in cause and effect."
Ralph Waldo Emerson

It is of ultimate importance at all times in our lives that we have a fundamental understanding of natural law and how it affects our lives. This is important at any time in our lives, but especially important in a time of grief. Understanding natural law will enable us to work with the laws and not against them. Understanding natural law will actually aid in our recovery.

Let me give an example of why it is important to understand natural law; we all understand how gravity works, that anything heavier than air, if dropped, will fall to the earth. Most have read or heard of a story of an infant who falls out of a window or crawls off of a balcony . . . the baby falls to his death. You may ask why God would let such a thing happen. God had nothing to do with it; a person in ignorance went directly against the law. There is not the slightest allowance for ignorance of the law. It was the baby's ignorance plus the parent's ignorance of the law that caused the baby's death. It did not happen by accident; it happened by natural law. Not understanding natural law can kill you.

I will name and describe the seven natural laws. Each law is important in itself, but all natural laws are connected and work together. I also want to mention that Emerson referred to one law as the law of laws—the Law of Cause and Effect.

In truth there is but one great law . . . ENERGY IS.

All physical and mental science is based on this one great law and its seven subsidiary laws which operate in coordination with each other.

The Seven Laws

1. The Law of Perpetual Transmission and Transmutation of Radiant Energy

Energy is constantly in a state of transmission and transmutation. Energy is moving into form, through form, and back into form.

On the scientific side, the law says that energy is. The law says that energy is neither created nor destroyed. It says that energy is always in motion and that the only difference is that energy changes from one form to another.

Theology says that God IS. That is as far as a true theologian can go. God is the cause and effect of himself, is neither created nor destroyed, and is 100 percent evenly present everywhere, always.

It is my opinion that science and theology agree. We have a great power that is evenly present everywhere, always. Energy is. God is. Why is that important to me? I believe with every fiber of my being that Cammie has simply changed forms. I believe Cammie is in a spiritual state in the present heaven. I also believe that I will see her again in the present heaven or in the new heaven and the new earth. This fact gives me much peace.

2. The Law of Relativity

The law of relativity states that everything is relative. It states that what is perceived as good or bad, healthy or unhealthy, tolerable or intolerable is all dependent on one's perception and the context in which it is seen.

We invoke the law of relativity almost every day. When we invoke the law of relativity we want to use it to our benefit and not to our detriment. Let me give you an example of invoking the law of relativity. Is an apple sweet or sour? If we compare an apple to a lemon, we may say the apple is sweet. If we compare an apple to sugar or honey, we may say the apple is sour. In reality the apple is neither sweet nor sour; it simply is, until we invoke the law of relativity.

This law of relativity helped me to keep Cammie's death in perspective and not let it spin out of control and become even worse than it was. Cammie's death was the biggest tragedy I have ever faced in life, but her *life* was one of the most valuable gifts I have ever been given. What is relative to me is her life. What a blessing! What a gift!

3. Law of Vibration

The law of vibration states that everything is in a constant state of movement. Everything vibrates. Nothing rests. Our bodies are changing at a rate of approximately fifty thousand cells per second. When someone says they have a "good vibe" about someone or something, they mean that they have a good feeling about the person or thing. In my recovery I have felt "good vibes" or "good vibrations" about a number of people and organizations. I knew I was vulnerable and was aware that untrustworthy people could make things worse, so I choose to listen to these "good vibrations" with much success. For example, I had good vibrations about Carmen when Debbie and I first met her and decided to accept her as my therapist. Conversely, I began to have "bad vibes" about one of my closest advisors. Upon doing some research, I found these "bad vibes" to be very accurate and subsequently terminated the services of this advisor.

The sub-law of the law of vibration is the Law of Attraction. This law states that we attract everything that comes into our lives, both the good and the bad, depending on what we think. We can either attract healing or be stuck in grief. It is our choice and we attract what we need to help us heal, through our thoughts, through our thinking. Thus, we need to constantly think about what we are thinking about.

I attracted incredible help from many places. Why was I attracting so much help into my life at that time? It was because of my thoughts. It was my thinking that was attracting everything and everyone I needed into my life, not only to heal, but to grow. It was the law of vibration and attraction at work. The thoughts I was thinking were thoughts of recovery. My overriding thoughts were of how significant Cammie's life had been and what I could do to honor her life. I can remember telling Carmen I wanted to find a way to honor Cammie's life. Carmen told me we would find ways to do that together and when we did, it would be significant. Honoring my daughter's life has been and continues to be my driving force. Honoring her by helping other hurting people—people in grief—has brought a new purpose and meaning to my life. My greatest prayer is that these ideas will help people to understand how our Creator put things together and how they can not only survive, but can also thrive.

4. The Law of Polarity or the Law of Opposites

Everything is up and everything is down, bad and good, hot and cold. You will never find one without finding the other. They are the opposite ends of the same things. They always come in pairs. You cannot have one without the other.

The law of polarity or law of opposites was a great help in my recovery. I knew the law stated that for every bad thing that comes into one's life, something good will also come. The law states that nothing ever stays the same, and that for every hot there will be a cold, for every bad there will be good, and for every valley, there will be a peak.

Cammie's death ushered in the biggest valley of my life. Immediately thereafter it was close to impossible for me to imagine ever coming out of this valley. It was hard to imagine that the sun would ever shine in my life again, but the **Son** did shine in my life. I could not visualize it right away but then I remembered the law . . . that for every bad there had to be a good. Without a doubt this was as bad as it could possibly ever get in my life; but I also remembered what the law stated and I knew something good had to come out of this as well.

I remember the first time Carmen told me that I would grow because of this process. That really made me angry. Carmen and I both can remember that night, but I grew to remember and came to an incredible new understanding of the law of polarity and how it works.

The growth and the healing would come to me, not because of Cammie's death, but because of her life and the way she lived it. The growth would come by honoring her. The growth came because of my thoughts.

5. The Law of Rhythm. Everything flows up and down, in and out.

This law operates on all three planes of understanding: intellectually, spiritually or emotionally, and physically

Intellectually there are days when you can solve a problem in a very short period of time. Then there are other days when the answers just won't come.

Spiritually there are days when you feel great, days when you can laugh and sing God's praises. Then there are other days when you feel down. You cannot laugh or sing or pray.

Physically there are days when you feel like you can move mountains. Other days you feel dragged out. You just want to curl up and be left alone.

This law operates on all three planes of understanding. It is working with you and with me this very moment.

The law of rhythm helped me to understand what was happening to me on all three planes of understanding, on the intellectual plane, the spiritual or emotional plane, and on the physical plane while I was in my deepest grief.

First I understood that there would be days when it would be difficult to concentrate on anything except my grief. There were days when I didn't want to get out of bed. There were days when everything seemed to run together. Nothing seemed to make any sense. I couldn't focus. I could barely function. I just wanted to crawl in a hole and be left alone. Then there would be other days when things seemed more normal. There were days when I could function; maybe not on the level I was accustomed to, but I could function on some level. I understood that that is how the law of rhythm works on an intellectual level. I began to look forward to the more normal days and focus on what my thoughts were on the high and low days. I understood that thoughts are things, and I was attracting how I felt with my thoughts. I was responsible for my thoughts and my thoughts were creating my feelings and actions.

Spiritually I was mad and glad. I was mad at God that Cammie was not here with me. I was mad at myself for not being able to recognize and understand all that was going on in her life. I was mad at myself and God for not being able to stop her from taking her life. There were days when it was difficult to pray. There were days when it was difficult to breathe. Then there were days that all I could feel was gratitude for the time I did have with Cammie. I was glad that she was my daughter and that I had had the privilege of being her father. Those were the days that I was able to thank God for her life, our time together, and the impact she had left on me and others.

Physically there were days when I felt washed out. I was at a physical low, and getting out of bed at five o'clock in the morning to exercise was all I could muster. I went through the motions, but my heart wasn't in it. I just felt like curling up in a fetal position. Then on other days I would be at a physical peak, looking forward to exercise because it felt good and I knew it would be a great stress reliever. How I looked forward to those days!

Understanding the law of rhythm helped me understand the rhythm of my grief and the rhythm of my recovery process.

6. The Law of Cause and Effect

Sir Isaac Newton describes the law of cause and effect on a physical plane with his third law of motion. The law states that for every action there is an equal and opposite reaction.

The law of cause and effect works exactly the same on the spiritual plane of life as on the physical plane of life. For example, before you can receive something of value, you have to give something of value. Before you can receive the gift of healing, you have to do the work of healing. If one is not willing to do the work of healing, the effect will be to remain stuck in grief. We live in a "give and take" universe. Emerson referred to the law of cause and effect as the Law of Laws.

If you are stuck in grief ask yourself these simple questions:

1. What am I doing to heal my mind?
2. What am I doing to heal my body?
3. What am I doing to heal my spirit?
4. Am I focused? Do I have a goal in recovery?
5. Am I dedicated? Do I have a burning desire to heal?
6. Am I disciplined? Am I doing the things I need to do to reach my goal of returning to wholeness?

When a loved one dies we typically feel sad and we grieve the loss. But, alternatively, the Law of Cause and Effect says that following the death of our loved ones, we can feel gratitude. If we think about the sense of entitlement we feel deserving of having our loved ones in our lives for a long period of time. We could feel victimized, even persecuted. If we think about our loved ones being on loan to us from God, the effect will be that we feel gratitude for the time that we did share while we were together here on this earth.

If you think you are sick, you will get sick. Psychosomatic illness is the most common illness being treated in our country today. Most doctors will say that at least fifty percent of all illness is psychosomatic. Some doctors will state much higher percentages. Conversely, if you think you can recover, you will recover. If you think you can heal, you will heal. If you think you can work through your grief back to wholeness, you will become whole again.

7. The Law of Gender or Law of Creation

The law of gender is often called the law of creation.

On a physical plane the law of gender decrees that every seed that's planted has a period of incubation. It takes a certain amount of time for that seed to be expressed in physical form in our world. We understand that a seed is planted with the sex act. Approximately 280 days later that seed expresses itself in the birth of a human being.

If you were to plant seeds of corn one day, you would not expect to have corn plants the next day. The law states that the plant will appear after a period of incubation. We understand that, so we do not plan the harvest until after the required number of days of incubation. That is how things occur on a physical plane.

The law of gender works exactly the same way on a spiritual level of understanding as it does on the physical plane. Whenever an idea or thought is planted in the mind, it takes a certain amount of time for that idea or thought to become manifest in our characters and to become a part of our souls.

When the seed of recovery is planted in us we *will* reap healing; we *will* reach wholeness.

All laws relate to one another.

1. The Law of Perpetual Transmission and Transmutation of Radiant Energy

2. The Law of Relativity

3. Law of Vibration

4. The Law of Polarity

5. The Law of Rhythm

6. The Law of Cause and Effect

7. The Law of Gender or Law of Creation

Some people would think it strange to talk about natural law in connection with grief and recovery, but for me it makes very good sense. In this chapter we discussed the seven natural laws. To truly understand the importance of natural laws and how those laws interact with one another in your own life, you will need to do some additional study and research on your own, as there is simply not enough time to cover the subject in one chapter.

To me the Seven Natural Laws can be stated simply as *the Natural Order of an Omnipotent God*. It truly is how God put things together in this marvelous universe, his creation. It is how he intended things to work together. If we are going to live and work and grow and heal, it makes sense to me to have at least a working knowledge of the laws that govern our universe. What an advantage it is for us to have an understanding of how God intended things to work together.

The incredible thing for me about coming to an understanding of natural law is how the laws dovetail with one another. It is not that one law depends upon another, but that all the laws are tied together in a beautiful dance. Each law is independent, yet dependent on all the others.

CHAPTER 28

GOD'S NATURAL LAWS

Carmen

"The greatest of all miracles is that we need not be tomorrow what
we are today, but we can improve if we make use of the potentials
implanted in us by God."
Samuel M. Silver

Larry said that learning about and understanding the seven natural
laws had made a huge difference in his life because they helped him
understand how life worked. He said that knowing about the seven
natural laws was like knowing the laws of life. He said they were
like having the rulebook to life. Larry had studied the seven natural
laws for most of his life and let me know that, second only to the
Bible, they were the single most important set of concepts he had
ever learned.

Once he began to regain his sanity, he said that thinking about
the seven natural laws was helping him in his recovery. I asked him
how that was helping him and he explained that just knowing that the
laws were always in effect helped him to stay grounded whether he
was in grief or not. The rules were always the rules. The laws were
always the laws. He said the laws helped him to remember how the
world worked even in grief when things seemed so chaotic. Life had
seemed so beyond his control for so much of his life in regard to the
suicides of his loved ones that the knowledge of the seven natural

laws helped life seem more organized and grounded, especially after the death of Cammie.

If there is a "secret" to healing from a traumatic loss, it is the healing of the mind, because how we think leads directly to how we feel. In the depths of grief we typically think about the great loss we have experienced. We think about how unjust the loss is and how unfair it is that we have to experience this loss. We think that the person is lost forever and we will never have contact with him or her again. We think that we will feel bad forever and will never be able to recover. We think that no one and nothing can ease our pain. We feel victimized and powerless over what has happened to us. We think that our lives will be dominated and defined by this great loss and that the loss will be the focus of our lives. We think that we may lose other things and we will not get the things we need. These thoughts lead us the two great human fears: fear we will lose what we have and the fear that we will not get what we want. These two great fears can lead us to feel depressed because we feel powerless over our current loss and about future losses and events.

Now the above typical grief thoughts are quite normal in the initial stages of grief and seem to come to us naturally as part of our defense mechanisms. However, these types of thoughts become highly dysfunctional if we hold on to them and make them the focus of our lives. These thoughts are the ones that keep us "stuck in grief."

With the powerful knowledge that our thoughts lead directly to how we feel, we can then change our thinking to thoughts of healing. Changing our loss focused thoughts to healing focused thoughts is called "reframing." We have the choice and the power to change our loss focused thoughts to healing focused thoughts. What kind of thoughts are healing focused thoughts? What kind of loss focused thoughts need to be reframed? Let's look at a few:

Loss focused thought:
The person I have lost is lost forever.

Reframed healing thought:
I have lost contact with my loved one physically here on earth, but I am still connected with my loved one spiritually.

Loss focused thought:
The death of my loved one is the worst thing that has ever happened to me.

Reframed healing thought:
The death of my loved one is painful, but the fact that I have been blessed with the presence of my loved one in my life at all far outweighs the fact that he or she died earlier than I would have preferred.

Loss focused thought:
No one will ever be able to help me heal from the pain of my loss.

Reframed healing thought:
I know that there will be people who will be glad to help me through my grief and I can be open to receiving that healing help. My thoughts will help me attract the help that I need.

Loss focused thought:
I will be down and depressed forever.

Reframed healing thought:
My feelings of being down and depressed are temporary, and I have power through my thoughts to change the way I feel at any time. I can choose to focus on the blessings in my life rather than the losses in my life whenever I want.

Loss focused thought:
This loss has wounded me so deeply, I am doomed to feel this profound pain forever, and no one can help me.

Reframed healing thought:
I can seek help for my grief, and if I work at my healing I will begin to feel better and my depression will lift.

Healing starts in the mind. It starts in our thoughts. We must always remember to think about what we are thinking about. Thoughts are things. We have a choice in the thoughts we choose. We can, we must choose healing focused thoughts.

CHAPTER 29

HEALING THE BODY

Larry

"The doctor of the future will give no medicine, but will interest his patients in the care of the human frame, in diet and in the cause and prevention of disease."
Thomas Edison

Up to this point we have talked about healing of the mind. Later in the book there will be a chapter on spirit. This chapter is about the body. The advice we are going to give you about taking care of your body is not intended to be optional. It is intended to be taken *literally*! It is *that* important.

Remember what Plato said, "There is no healing until you have healed mind, body, and spirit."

When there is great grief in your life one of the first things to go is your health. I was sick for months after Cammie died. Before that I was very seldom ill. This happened to me. This happens to most people following the death of a loved one.

Another thing that often happens when someone in your life dies is that your weight changes. Your weight goes up or your weight goes down, but in most cases it does change. The reason for the change is that you are either not eating or you are eating too much. You eat all the comfort food that people bring and you gain weight, or else you eat nothing and you lose weight. All of this is brought about by your great sadness, your grief. After Cammie died, even with an exercise program, I gained twenty pounds as I indulged in the comfort food.

Before Cammie died I had maintained a rigorous exercise program, consistently working out one hour a day, six days a week. This was an important part of my life, a wonderful stress reliever that kept me in shape for my annual "extreme exercise vacations."

During the evening of the day that Cammie died my priest Merrill Wade was at our home. The last thing he told me to do before leaving for the evening was to rest and to get up at five o'clock in the morning for my exercise routine. Merrill said that I would cry all through the workout, but it was very important to maintain my exercise program. He had the wisdom to know that exercise would be a great stress reliever and that the chemicals released could be as effective as taking antidepressant medication. He knew that I needed to maintain my workout discipline. He knew I needed to maintain a disciplined life, and the exercise would help a great deal more than even I understood at the time. He knew that the exercise would strengthen me for the challenges that lay ahead.

What are the things you need to do to maintain your health when someone you love dies? You need to maintain good nutrition, get enough rest, and exercise daily. You need to stay hydrated as water is essential to life, most especially at this point in your life. These are not easy things to do when you are in the midst of your great sadness. Grieving the death of a loved one takes its toll on one's body. This is true no matter what the cause of death, but especially so in the event of a sudden and unexpected death.

Exercise, nutrition, and commitment are essential. Focus, dedication, and commitment will be required to maintain an exercise program in your grief. It is five o'clock in the morning and you can't sleep. What do you do? If you did not have an exercise regimen before the death of your loved one, it is one of the most important things you can do for your recovery, for your survival. Think of exercise as survival training in grief. Exercise is that important! It's your new job. Exercise is one of the most important *tools* you can use to help yourself heal.

Remember what Plato said, "There is no healing until you have healed mind, body, and spirit." The body is the temple! A gift from

God and we are the stewards of that gift. We need to be good stewards and take good care of our bodies. Remember T→F→A, thoughts cause feelings that cause actions. We get to *choose* our state of health! What I have learned about exercise and the body while being on this journey has been phenomenal. I know now that exercise helped save my life. Before being on this grief journey, I thought I knew the importance of exercise and how it can help relieve stress; but now I am a real believer. I know beyond a shadow of a doubt that exercise was a key factor in my ability to recover.

Maintaining my exercise program was and is an important discipline in my life. Discipline in one's life is always important, but when a person is in extreme grief, any sense of normalcy or discipline is of utmost importance. Just the fact that it gives you something to do at a given time for a given period of time each day is important. In the beginning stages of extreme grief, your whole world is lived in a kind of fog. Having something to do as important as exercise at a specific time each day is something you can actually look forward to. Yes, I said look forward to and, at this point in your life, there is not much of that around!

The chemicals that are released during a vigorous workout routine help not only with your stress at that moment, but throughout the rest of the day. The feeling is kind of like a "runner's high." If you are sick in mind, body, and spirit all at the same time, the toll it takes on you is enormous and it makes your recovery just that much harder. Maintaining a vigorous exercise program will shorten your recovery period.

Recovery is a battle for your life. If you are going to send someone into battle, you want him to be in good physical condition so that he will have the strength and endurance for the fight. In this case you are the warrior and the life you are trying to save is your own. The world you are trying to restore is your world. Exercise helps give you that strength and endurance, the stamina to tolerate the journey, the journey back to wholeness.

CHAPTER 30

HEALING EXERCISE

Carmen

"Lack of activity destroys the good condition of every human being, while movement and methodical physical exercise save it and preserve it."
Plato

Most teachers will tell you that they learn more from their students than their students learn from them. Likewise most therapists will tell you that they learn as much from their patients as their patients learn from them, and I am no exception. I learned many things from Larry, but one of the most important was the component of healing that is often minimized, overlooked, or ignored: the healing of the body.

When I was first introduced to Larry I was told that there was concern about him because he was exercising daily so soon after the death of his child. I remember thinking that this was an interesting concern and one that I had not heard before. Of all the concerns one could have about a griever, this was one that was not usually very high on the list of priorities following the death of a loved one. I just filed this concern away in my mind until I had more information.

Later on Larry told me the place exercise had in his life and how it was helping him survive the death of his daughter. He told me about his lifelong practice of exercising regularly and about his commitment to helping himself stay healthy. He was actually known for his commitment to being physically fit. Larry related the story of his priest getting in his face the day of the death of Cammie and telling him to continue his exercise routine no matter what and how he followed that advice. Larry told me how continuing to exercise was helping him to stay strong enough to deal with the stress of his daughter's death.

Now anyone can use any behavior or substance addictively following the death of a loved one to cope with the stress and pain, and for a therapist, this was something for which to screen. But as I questioned Larry about his use of exercise, it was clear that he was not using it addictively; he was using it as one of many coping mechanisms to survive the blow of Cammie's death. He explained his philosophy of healing and his awareness of the need to incorporate mind, body, and spirit in the healing process.

Larry said that he did not know much and had no idea how he would be able to survive his child's death, but what he did know was that he would need to be physically strong to do the work that would be needed, and that was one thing over which he had control.

To this day, Larry continues to exercise, continues to heal, continues to spread the word about the role of physical health in the healing process and continues to inspire others to incorporate fitness into their grief survival strategy. I knew of Plato's statement that, "There is no healing until you have healed mind, body, and spirit." I even had it on my list of favorite quotes, but not until observing Larry's life experience and the effect I saw it having on his healing, did I realize how truly important that three-part healing strategy was. Larry took Plato's advice literally and I saw firsthand the powerful effect it had on his healing. I will never minimize or underestimate the role of exercise in healing after seeing how it helped Larry. I will always remember to take Plato's words literally that there truly is no healing "until you have healed mind, body, and spirit."

CHAPTER 31

HEALING THE SPIRIT

Larry

"Until a man is nothing, God can make nothing out of him."
Martin Luther

First I want to say that after Cammie died, I was mad at God. I think this would be a natural reaction for anyone. I also think it is OK. Yes, I think it is OK to get mad at God. I think we have a God who is big enough to take my getting mad at him and to understand and still love me. That is just my opinion and I thought you needed to know. I sure hope I am right.

I believe that spiritual healing is different for each individual. The only thing I can convey to you is how I was touched spiritually and where I was and where I am now on my spiritual walk. This journey has been a spiritual awakening. The love and gratitude that was shown and poured out to Debbie and me through this whole experience has been and continues to be overwhelming.

The only way I can convey this is from a Christian perspective. I'm a Christian. Please understand that when I say that I am a Christian, I am not speaking it with pride, but rather confessing that I stumble and I need someone to guide me. When I say that I am a Christian I am not saying that I am strong, but professing that I am weak and I need to pray for strength every day in order to make it through the day. I am not bragging of success; I am admitting I failed. I am not claiming to be perfect. My flaws are far too visible. But God believes I'm worth it and I know I am loved.

I am not a member of the clergy, nor have I ever been to seminary. I am not a theologian. I am a layperson who has spent many years in Bible studies, and I do spend time in prayer each day. Prayer has made a tremendous difference in my life. Prayer has made a tremendous difference in my journey back to wholeness. Prayer has made a tremendous difference in my spiritual healing.

My prayer time has become much more important to me since Cammie died. I talk to God every day. I have come to understand in the middle of my great sadness that prayer does not change God. It changes my spirit. Prayer changes me, and I needed to change.

I have several prayers that I say every day. I can count on one hand the days that I have not said these prayers in the last twenty years. These are very special prayers to me. I have spent many hours meditating on each line and on every word of the prayers and how they affect my life and my relationship with God. These prayers are printed at the end of this chapter. I hope you find them useful.

I have come to understand that when Jesus gave us the Lord's Prayer he was teaching us how to pray. He taught us to acknowledge God as our loving Father and Lord. He taught us that things can and should be done here on earth not just in heaven. He taught us to ask for our basic needs, to ask for forgiveness, to forgive others, and to ask for help in dealing with the stresses and pitfalls of life.

I have an image of God as Abba Father. I can see myself curling up in his lap with his loving arms around me, telling me I'm going to be made whole. I can also see his loving arms around Cammie, welcoming her into the present heaven. I know I will see her again. This is faith at work.

My baby girl is dead. I needed to come to an understanding of where she was and what was happening to her. A general understanding of that was adequate before but now I needed specifics.

The essence of my spiritual healing included the people and events with which God continued to bless Debbie and me on a daily basis. To me this has been an incredible illustration of how God works in natural law. God's natural law of vibration, law of attraction, has never been more evident in my life. I knew I needed help. I desperately wanted to survive, and I truly think that the vibrations that I transmitted somehow caused everything and everyone I needed to be attracted into my life.

Spiritual healing happened to me through a series of events that could have only been orchestrated by a loving God. Let me give you some examples. At seven o'clock the morning after Cammie died, I called Fran Moss. She was at our house at 7:30 a.m. First let me say that to be blessed with an incredibly talented friend like Fran who loves you deeply and who wants to express her love to you can only be a gift from God. Fran suspended all other personal activities and made helping Debbie and me the top priority in her life.

Fran was there to help with the planning of the funeral and the celebration of Cammie's life. Fran was there to help and support us through the entire process. She was at the funeral home with the family on Saturday and with friends and family on Sunday evening. Having the foresight to know that this day would be one of the most horrendous days of our lives, Fran took charge. She knew how to take care of difficult situations and people while still being loving and considerate of everyone's feelings at such an emotional time.

This incredible angel continued to guide and lead us for the days and weeks and months to come. The Sunday after Cammie's funeral Fran called to say she was bringing us breakfast. She arrived with a spectacular array of food and china. There was an egg casserole, fresh fruit, oatmeal, juice, coffee, sweet cinnamon rolls, dishes, mugs, napkins and all the needed utensils. My question is how can someone be so thoughtful and love you so much and you not see this as a gift from God? God had sent us an angel called Fran to gently guide us through this process.

Bob and Glynda Reames, our close friends that live in Arlington, Texas, came to Austin the day after Cammie died so they could be close to us. They spent the first night with their daughter, who lives in Austin. Then Debbie and I requested that they stay with us. They said they were hoping we would ask. They were with us for the next five days and nights. They were there to care for us. They were a tremendous blessing.

This is how spiritual healing started. It started with God's church, his people, the body of Christ alive in the world. There to offer and take care of our every need. There to be a shoulder to cry on and there to hold us up when we could not stand alone.

MORNING PRAYER

Oh God,
For another day,
For another morning,
For another hour,
For another minute,
For another chance to live and serve thee,
I am truly grateful.
Do thou this day free me from
All fear of the future,
From all anxiety about tomorrow,
From all bitterness toward anyone,
From all cowardliness in the face of danger,
From all laziness in the face of work,
From all failure before opportunity,
From all weakness when thy power is at hand.
But fill me with love that knows no barrier,
With sympathy that reaches to all,
With courage that cannot be shaken,
With faith strong enough for the darkness,
With strength sufficient for my task,
With loyalty to thy kingdom's goal,
With wisdom to meet life's complexities,
With power to lift me to thee,
Be thou with me for another day,
And use me as thou wilt.
Amen
Author unknown

A GENERAL THANKSGIVING

Father God,
Accept, O Lord, our thanks and praise
for all that you have done for us.
We thank you for the splendor of the whole creation,
for the beauty of this world,
for the wonder of life,
and for the mystery of love.
We thank you for the blessing of family and friends
and for the loving care which surrounds us on each side.
We thank you for setting us at tasks which demand our best effort,
and for leading us to accomplishments which satisfy and delight us.
We thank you also for those disappointments and failures
that lead us to acknowledge our dependence on you alone.
Above all, we thank you for your Son Jesus Christ;
for the truth of his word
and the example of his life;
for his steadfast obedience, by which he overcame temptation;
for his dying, through which he overcame death;
and for his rising to life again,
in which we are raised to life in your kingdom.
Grant us the gift of your Spirit,
that we may know Christ and make him known;
and through him, at all times and in all places,
may give thanks to you in all things.
Amen

The Book of Common Prayer[5]

CHAPTER 32

HEALING PRAYER

Carmen

"They that wait upon the Lord shall renew their strength; they shall mount up with wings as eagles; they shall run, and not be weary; and they shall walk, and not faint."
Isaiah 40:31 KJV

As I got to know Larry better, I began to see some patterns of behavior he brought into his recovery. Larry had a number of helpful things he did daily and had done them for many years. These behaviors included engaging in daily prayer, exercising, being grateful, thought stopping, working on his current goal, reading positive literature, attending church on Sundays, and communicating with his wife and circle of friends. All of these behaviors were healthy, brought him pleasure, fed his mind, body, and spirit, maintained balance in his life, and significantly strengthened his resiliency.

Balance

Larry was a literalist, had high self-esteem, and had developed great discipline in that when he read or heard about things that were good for his mind, body, or spirit, he would integrate them into his lifestyle. Though many people do this to some degree, Larry would commit to these things with a very high degree of consistency, and would do them whether he felt like it or not, because he believed they were good for him.

Reframing—on a daily basis

Larry told me he had prayed the same daily prayers for twenty years. Every day for twenty years he had expressed his gratitude to God, asked for wisdom, asked for strength to do his will, asked for courage to change what he could, and asked God to strengthen him so that he could accept the things he could not change. Larry would thank God for each and every blessing in his life. He truly was thankful for everything he had received in his life.

I observed that Larry enjoyed praying. He appeared to have an innate spirituality. Larry had attended his beloved Episcopal church for many years, but it was my impression that his spirituality came from his heart of gratitude rather than merely from an institution. Larry's spirit was fed whenever he went to his church, and he drew strength from praising and thanking God and from fellowship with his fellow parishioners.

Conscious contact with God on a daily basis

I asked Larry if his spirituality had been affected by Cammie's death. He said he was shaken but not shaken to the core, but the "whys" and "hows" of the fourth and most shattering of the suicidal deaths into his life flooded into his mind. Why did God let this happen? Why didn't God stop it? Why would a loving God let his little girl suffer? How could God let suicide happen again for a fourth time in his life?

Larry said he had all of these questions he wanted to ask God. He was angry at God for allowing this to happen. But even though his faith was shaken, one constant he knew was that God would be there to help him through it all. He could literally see God helping him through people and situations in his life that he could not have orchestrated for himself. It was like God was sending him important and powerful gifts every week, if not every day, that were helping him through his grief and his restoration. Somehow Larry knew that even in all of this overwhelming sadness, God was, indeed, very good.

The reframe of gratitude

Larry's use of the tool of gratitude was striking to me. I was struck by the fact that he was able to feel such tremendous gratitude in the middle of the greatest anguish and sorrow he had ever experienced in his life. He felt the pain fully and never tried to skirt the pain. He knew he could not skip the step of feeling his feelings of agony, but he also realized that he could feel the feelings of gratitude and pain at the same time.

Whenever a person experiences the death of a beloved person, the feelings of sorrow, the feelings of loneliness, and the feelings of abandonment are the primary feelings a person experiences. These feelings are agonizing, overwhelming, and intense. Some people say they feel guilty if they do not continue to feel these hurtful feelings. They often will say that they feel like they are not honoring their loved ones if they begin to have feelings of gratitude and joy. If the feelings of gratitude and joy begin to overshadow the feelings of sorrow, people often will say that they feel conflicted because of the fear that others will accuse them of not caring about their loved ones enough. The myth that feeling happy again is proof that love for the loved one is shallow is very prevalent in our society today and plays a huge part in perpetuating the concept that eternal grief is the only form of honorable grief for someone we love.

Focus—on the death or on the life of a loved one

Larry felt these conflicted feelings at first, but then as his strength and his sanity returned he found himself experiencing profound feelings of gratitude for Cammie as a gift to him rather than feeling bitter because she was "taken" from him much sooner than he would have liked. Larry also came to the profound spiritual realization that he did not own Cammie and that he never had owned her. He felt gratitude that she had been on loan to him by God for thirty-nine years. He felt gratitude that God had allowed him the privilege of being her father while she was here on earth. He felt gratitude for the quality time he had been fortunate enough to have with her while she was here. He felt gratitude for the great joy Cammie had brought into his life. He felt gratitude for the closeness and love he experienced with this beautiful child. He felt gratitude for all of the memories he had of his life with Cammie, memories that could never be taken away and would be with him always.

Focus on memories rather that death

Larry said the Reverend Susan Barnes told him that gratitude was the best medicine anyone could take for healing. Larry seemed to know that feeling gratitude was as healing as any medicine he could have been given.

Prior to Cammie's death, Larry had a long history of giving thanks every day for the many blessings in his life. He had given thanks for the previous twenty years of his life for the multitude of gifts he had received from God. Gratitude was a habit Larry practiced all day every day for most of his life. He truly was a man of great appreciation and gratitude because he believed that the gifts bestowed upon a person were given by the grace of a loving God. He believed that man did not earn or even deserve the gifts that God gave to him. He believed that everything a person received in life was given to him by God. Larry also believed in hard work and doing his part. He understood that "God helps those who help themselves," but that whether a person worked hard or not, anything that came to a person was given to that person by grace. He believed that God owed us nothing, and that anything we happen to have in life is truly a gift from God.

Focus on gratitude is authentic, genuine and realistic

I wondered if taking the medicine of gratitude all of his life was what had helped Larry get through all of the previous deaths by suicide in his family. I wondered how it could not have helped him. Something had strengthened him to survive these massive losses. The losses were so great that it almost seemed as if something supernatural had been fortifying him all those years. I wondered if that strength might have come from his lifelong attitude of gratitude.

CHAPTER 33

UNDERSTANDING THE "FIRSTS"

Larry

"You can clutch the past so tightly to your chest that is leaves your
arms too full to embrace the present."
Jan Glidewell

By "The Firsts" I mean the first time something happens, or the first
special date or holiday that happens after the death of your loved
one. The firsts can be very painful. They can push every button you
have and absolutely bring you to your knees again and again without
advanced notice. But it does not have to be that way with some
forethought and planning and just the realization that this is part of
the grief process. The balance of this chapter will describe many of
my "firsts" and how I dealt with them, both good and bad.

The first Thanksgiving

The first Thanksgiving after Cammie's death was about a week after
her funeral. I found very little to give thanks for. I was still very much
in a fog and in very deep grief and actually remember very little
about that first Thanksgiving. You see, sometimes the "first" happens
so soon that it is not like a first at all, because you are just too numb.
What really seemed like the first Thanksgiving was a year later.

Thanksgiving was a special holiday for Cammie and for Debbie and me. We loved preparing the food. We loved the extra time we could spend with each other. We always had a lot to be thankful for. We loved being with family, and not having Cammie with us that second year after her death seemed like a "first" to us.

Seeing a car like Cammie's for the first time

Cammie drove a white Scion. A Scion looks like a box on four tiny wheels. She loved that car. She drove to Wyoming and back in it and talked about how comfortable it was. I had my doubts. That being said, every time I see a white Scion I have to see who is driving it. I know it sounds nuts, but I keep thinking I will find one with Cammie behind the wheel.

A friend of Debbie's was delivering food to our house after Cammie's death. I happened to be in the driveway when she pulled in. She looked very much like Cammie and was driving a white Scion. I was frozen in the driveway and burst into tears. Debbie had to explain to her friend that this was the first time I had seen a white Scion since Cammie died.

The first Christmas

The first Christmas for us was six weeks following Cammie's funeral. We decided not to decorate that year because it was just too soon, we needed time to heal, and all the trappings of Christmas would have been too painful. Even the next year we only partially decorated. It was not until our third Christmas without Cammie that we were able to decorate, have people in our home, and really share the joy of the season. There was simply no joy in that first Christmas.

The first time back at church

I love our church, but I have to say that the first time back in the sanctuary where we had held the celebration of her life was very painful. I had a hard time concentrating because all I could think about was Cammie and what had gone on in this holy place just a few days before. Concentrating on the sermon was very difficult. I remember that I couldn't sing, because there was no song in my heart. Being greeted by friends who had the greatest intention of saying the right things felt awkward to me. The ones who really understood just held us and cried with us.

Seeing another father with his daughter for the first time

People normally sit in the same pews every Sunday. I don't know why this happens, but it does. Debbie and I are no different. There is a couple at church who always sit within one or two rows of us every Sunday. Their daughter, son-in-law, and twin boys had moved back to Austin. The first time I turned around in church to pass the peace, greet our fellow parishioners, and saw his beautiful dark-haired daughter, who reminded me so much of Cammie, standing next to him, I lost it. All kinds of things were going through my mind . . . how much I missed Cammie and how unfair it seemed that he had his daughter next to him and I couldn't have mine next to me. We had to change where we sat on Sunday for a while because it was just too painful to be that close to another father and daughter who I know have such a special relationship. It reminded me too much of Cammie and me. Cammie had sat with me in that same pew the Sunday before she died. We were so proud to have Cammie with us that one Sunday, and now it all seemed too unfair.

We have now moved back to our "old" pew, and with time and some hard work I can tolerate and even enjoy watching this daughter interact with her father and children. I have grown to know her and her husband and I have noticed that she has the same sweet spirit that Cammie had, and I can be happy for them and enjoy them myself.

First dinner party

Several weeks into our great sadness we thought we were ready to accept an invitation to a small dinner party. What struck me as odd was that none of our friends mentioned Cammie. Not one. These were the same friends who had come to our rescue and now did not even mention her name. I guess that they were trying to "protect" us, but it seemed very awkward. The greatest tragedy of our life was unfolding before our eyes and no one mentioned it. It seemed surreal.

The first birthday after Cammie's death

Cammie's first birthday after her death was a major event for Debbie and me. In retrospect, what seems strange was that it was not a major event for anyone else, including our family members. No one in our family mentioned Cammie's birthday.

Because I had been in therapy for several months, I was healing at what felt like a steady pace, but the advent of Cammie's birthday was a major event in my life. I felt like I was back at square one. I did not feel rational. Before this year we were usually with Cammie on her birthday. We would take her to dinner and get to spend some quality time with her. This year was going to be different. The birthday was still here, but Cammie wasn't.

My heart was breaking. How do I celebrate my child's birthday when she is not here to celebrate with me? Carmen suggested that we should still celebrate Cammie's birthday, but that we needed a plan for the day. Our plan was a simple one. On the morning of Cammie's birthday, Debbie and I took several large red helium-filled balloons to her gravesite. We wrote messages to Cammie on each balloon before we released them into the clouds. We told her we loved her. We told her we missed her. Debbie wrote, "I know you are dancing with angels." When the balloons ascended into the clouds we both felt that we were communicating directly with Cammie. It was truly a high and holy moment for Debbie and me. We also left a large heart-shaped Mylar helium-filled balloon that said "Happy Birthday" at the gravesite.

One other thing that I did which may not seem like a high and holy moment to anyone else was this: Cammie loved a cold "Bud Lite" and on this hot summer day in July, I took her a cold "Bud Lite." I know this may sound corny, but I opened it and poured it on her grave while saying, "Honey, this Bud's for you!" Somehow all of these things brought us a great deal of peace. Somehow we felt Cammie's presence; doing these things helped us feel close to her. We had celebrated her birthday and spent some quality time with her. Carmen was right on both counts. We needed to celebrate, but the celebration had to be planned. Celebrating important dates is a must, but the celebration must be planned.

The first anniversary of Cammie's death

By this time I had been in therapy for eleven months and was really feeling good. I felt that a lot of healing had taken place. I was working through the grief and gradually returning to wholeness, but the advent of the first anniversary of my baby girl's death really knocked me off my feet. For about two weeks leading up to the day, I was becoming increasingly crazy. I felt insane again. I was having trouble coping. I wondered what was happening to me and had not yet tied this to the approaching anniversary. I was scared. I felt like I was back at square one and maybe it simply wasn't possible to heal from this type of grief. Maybe I was just fooling myself. I stopped using my tools. The grief was overwhelming. It was as if Cammie had just died and I was going through everything again. It was agony. What could I do?

Once again, it was Carmen and Debbie to the rescue. Debbie sent me with a list of things to discuss with Carmen. Debbie wanted to know what was happening to me too. This was a very trying time for both of us. When I told Carmen what was happening to me she told me I was not going crazy, that I was still healing, but that the anniversary of my daughter's death was coming soon and was a major event in the life of any father who had experienced the sudden and traumatic death of his child.

Once again Carmen talked about the importance of planning for this important event. She asked what things would be comforting to us. What things would bring us peace and healing? We planned the day to truly celebrate Cammie's life, to celebrate the gift she had been to us. With Carmen's, Debbie's, and Fran's help we planned a full day of events to honor our child.

The day went like this. Debbie and I started the day off by meeting Fran and her golden retriever for what turned out to be a hike in the woods. Unbeknownst to Fran, she had suggested a place to meet that turned out to be very significant to me. The park she suggested just happened to be located on the very same road where my father had lived as a small child. It was also the same road where the small community cemetery was located and where my father was buried. After a couple of hours of hiking in the woods we decided to visit my father's grave. This felt wonderful because it somehow tied Cammie and Dad together, and I felt close to both of them.

After a light lunch, we went to a nursery and purchased sixty pansies to surround the monument at Cammie's gravesite. Later we would find out from Cammie's maternal grandmother that pansies were Cammie's favorite flower. What a God coincidence it was to know that my baby girl would be surrounded by her favorite flower. Lisa Bargsley, a close friend of ours, calls this a "God Wink." There were a lot of those that day. The simple act of kneeling to till the soil and plant the pansies turned out to be very healing. I felt God's presence and healing touch throughout the entire day. We truly celebrated Cammie's life all day long and it was good! It truly was a celebration worthy of my princess. By the way, the pansies looked beautiful and I also took her another "Bud Lite." Once again we needed to celebrate, but the celebration needed to be planned in advance.

All the anxiety, all the grief, all the fear, all the agony I had felt for the preceding two weeks had vanished. I felt like I had been blessed; we had turned a horrible day, the worst day of my life, into a celebration of my child's life. Once again God was showing us and teaching us about gifts. What a gift that day was! That day and its events would prove to be a major turning point in my healing.

We have now turned this into an annual event and invite special friends to join us on this special day of celebration. We meet at the cemetery ready to till the soil, plant the pansies, and celebrate Cammie's life. What a gift!

Hearing "Do you have children?" for the first time

Preparation is important. Carmen and I had discussed the inevitable question that would sooner or later come up. The question could come up in a social gathering or in a business meeting, but sooner or later someone was going to ask the question, "Do you have children?" Even though I had prepared my response by talking this out with Carmen before it ever happened the first time, the question still came as a great shock.

I was having lunch at a nice restaurant with a person from my office and a new vendor with whom I was negotiating. We were going through all the small talk people do when they are trying to build a new relationship. You want to indicate to the other person that you are really interested in building a personal relationship with them, not just a business relationship. Everything was going fine. The vendor was talking about his children and then it happened. He asked the question, that dreaded question that I knew someday would come. "Do you have children?" I remember my colleague looking at me as though I might pass out. I had tears in my eyes and was trying to catch my breath. The question had taken my breath away and just about stopped my already broken heart. There was a long pregnant pause before I could answer. He was very gracious and said, "If there is something wrong you don't need to answer the question." I remember how I answered him. I thanked him for being gracious and then explained, "I have two children. I have a daughter and four beautiful grandchildren who live in Waco. I have a second daughter. The reason your question took my breath away is that this is the first time this question has been asked of me since my youngest daughter died in November of last year."

We briefly discussed the details of Cammie's life and death. Of course he offered his condolences. I remember the sincerity of his response when he told me that he didn't know how anyone could endure this kind of pain and grief. He told me that he did not know if he could endure the death of one of his children. He commented on the strength it must have taken to answer his question. He was shocked at my ability to still be functioning since it had only been about six months since Cammie's death.

The preparation was important. Even with the preparation, even knowing the inevitable fact that this question would be asked, it still took my breath away. Without the preparation, it would have knocked me off my feet. I was still very vulnerable and it took very little for my emotions to come to the surface.

I was fortunate. I had a gracious understanding person with whom to experience this "first." You may not be as fortunate as I was. That is why preparation . . . talking about, talking through, and anticipating things that will happen . . . is so very important. Preparation is a must.

The first time you wake up and realize it is not a dream

I do not remember the first time this "first" actually happened. But this "first" doesn't happen just once. It happens repeatedly and each time it seems like a "first." This happens to everyone. I have never talked to anyone who has not had this experience. It is a strange feeling. This happened frequently after Cammie died. I would awaken in the middle of the night or in the morning or after a short catnap and the sensation was always the same. I opened my eyes to a brief moment of hope, of joy that this is all a dream. This has to be a dream. How could my beautiful daughter be dead? How could my beautiful daughter have taken her own life?

As much as I want to stay in denial, as much as I want this to be a dream, as much as I want to stay in this dream, it is not. Harsh reality rushes in. Then I realize this is not a dream. This is a nightmare; it is real and I will never wake up from it.

This is part of grief. Coming to an acceptance and understanding that I am not losing touch with reality is very important. Waking up and realizing it is not a dream is part of the grief process. Even though this hurts, for a brief moment, it does feel like a dream and I have a moment of joy. Many times I have cried myself back to sleep. This still happens today. Don't be surprised when this happens to you. Be happy about the brief moment of joy. It is a gift!

Seeing little girls for the first time

Anyone who has a daughter knows what I mean when I say, "Your baby girl will always be your baby girl." Even though Cammie was thirty-nine when she died, she was still my baby girl. When she was alive I would see young girls who would remind me of Cammie and it would put a smile on my face. After her death it was different because it would bring tears rather than a smile.

It always seems to happen at the most inopportune times. It has happened at church, at the grocery store, in department stores, and on airplanes. I see a dark-haired, brown-eyed little girl and the tear ducts go to work. Initially it brings back fond memories of when Cammie was a little girl, but it also brings back the realization that she is not with me anymore. After the tears, there is still the moment of joy remembering my little girl.

This continues to happen. With time, I am better able to deal with these situations, but it does not stop them from happening and I am glad that it doesn't. Even though there is pain, there is still joy in remembering Cammie and seeing other little girls interact with their fathers. When this first happened, my reaction was so obvious that on several occasions I had to explain why this was happening to me. Time has eased the pain of these situations and intensified the joy. The joy far outweighs the pain.

This happens to me. Chances are this will happen to you. My point in telling you this is to prepare you for the inevitable pain, but to also help you realize and understand that the joy outweighs the pain. I don't go looking for these situations, but I don't run away either. In all honesty I wish it could all be only a fond recollection, but I will take the moments of joy, even when mixed with pain, and cherish them.

Hearing her recorded voice for the first time

The first time I heard Cammie's recorded voice was several days or weeks after she died. To tell the truth, I cannot recall exactly. I called her home to talk to her husband about meeting him at the cemetery, and he was not home. Cammie's voice was still on the voice mail greeting. What a shock hearing her voice. It hurt like hell. It felt good. I wanted to hang up and call again just to hear her voice again. The shock of hearing her voice and knowing that she was dead was surreal. I did not call back after that. I left the husband a message. It brought up too much pain; it pushed every button I had. Hearing her voice and knowing I could never talk to her again was too much to bear.

I know some people continue to keep a deceased child's voice on their voice mail greetings on home phones or cell phones for long periods of time. I have been told they get comfort from hearing the voice and if this brings them one moment of joy, I can see why it would be worth it to them. For me, it was too soon. For me, all I could concentrate on was her death, the fact that she was not with me anymore, the fact that she would not be with me anymore. As much as I wanted to hear her voice, I did not want it to be a recording. I wanted it to be her voice. I did not call her home again after that. I don't think there is a right or wrong in this situation. Whatever feels right for you is what you should do. Follow your heart. For me her recorded voice was haunting.

At some point during the funeral preparation, one of Cammie's in-laws gave me a copy of a CD that Cammie had cut. I took it home, put it in a desk drawer, and looked at it every few months. It stayed there almost two years before I could bring myself to listen to it. I do not know what I was afraid of. I was so affected by hearing her voice on the telephone recording that I was really frightened at what might happen when I heard her singing on the CD.

When I played the CD the first time, I did it when I was alone. I was concerned about what my reaction might be. The recording caused a flood of emotion. I had no idea what kind of songs Cammie had recorded. As it turned out, all of the songs were religious songs she sang in church. I knew that she sang a lot of solos at church, but had no idea that she had made a recording. When I heard the CD, I realized that this was a professional recording complete with background accompaniment and mixing. What a shock to hear my baby's beautiful voice. There were many tears. There was a lot of emotion. Trying to understand how Cammie could have sung these songs with so much joy and conviction and then have gotten to such a low point that she was able to take her own life was difficult to comprehend. How could this have happened to my beautiful baby girl?

Cammie's faith was strong. The songs she sang revealed her faith and her yearning to be closer to God. The songs revealed her expectation of being with God in heaven and how peaceful it would be. I heard hope in her voice. Where did that hope go? How did she become so hopeless? The songs she sang painted a beautiful picture of being with God. I know she is. I just didn't expect her to be there so soon.

CHAPTER 34

MOMENTS OF JOY

Carmen

"I know God will not give me anything I can't handle. I just wish
that He didn't trust me so much."
Mother Teresa

Even though Larry had experienced four suicides in his immediate
family, he, like many others, was unfamiliar with the grief process
and the technicalities of how the process worked, especially with
regard to the part called the "firsts." Many people are caught off guard
regarding the "firsts" because they are not prepared for experiencing
them. When they begin happening, the "firsts" can hit a person
without advance notice and hit him hard and sometimes lead him
to feel like he is going "insane." I decided to tell Larry about this
phenomenon called the "firsts" so that at least he would not be caught
off guard. I wanted him to be armed with knowledge about how the
"firsts" worked.

The "firsts" have the potential to re-traumatize those of us in
grief because they trigger fond memories and painful memories
simultaneously. They trigger our brains to remember wonderful
memories about our loved ones and then slam us with the knowledge
that our loved ones will never be available here on earth to enjoy these
times with us in the present or in the future. For example, the first
holiday such as Christmas can occur following the death a loved one

and we are flooded with wonderful memories of all of the holidays together in the past, and then our brains begin to think about the current holiday and instantly realizes that the loved ones are not here with us and there will be no future Christmases celebrated together in the future. So we go from the "high" of the good memories and instantly descend into the agonizingly painful depths of the current reality that we are alone in the holiday and our loved ones will not be joining us like before.

Because there are so many "firsts," they assault us over and over again during that first year, and we are often helpless to understand what is happening to us and why we keep hurting so badly. Interestingly enough, just having knowledge that the "firsts" exist and will be happening following the death of a loved one can prepare us to deal with them effectively. Planning and preparation for how to deal with the "firsts" when the time comes can arm us with a powerful set of tools and can dilute the tremendous shock effect the "firsts" can have when we are unarmed.

And so I warned Larry about the "firsts," and he said he appreciated knowing about them and began to look out for them. Larry reported that the awareness of the "firsts" helped him deal with them more effectively as they no longer had the power of surprise. As the "firsts" began happening to him, he would say to himself things like, "Ouch, that hurt, it was one of those 'firsts again, but I am not slipping back in my recovery, I am not insane, and this pain is only temporarily acute and will pass. I can focus on the joy of these moments rather than the pain."

CHAPTER 35

A MARRIAGE CAN SURVIVE

Larry

"A team is two or more people with two things in common: a
shared goal and good communication."
Chuck Bowman

When a child dies, many marriages do not survive. One study
cited statistics stating that as high as 80 percent to 90 percent of all
marriages after the death of a child end in divorce. Why is this? Why
do marriages that may have been very strong before the death of a
child end in divorce? What happens?

I don't have the answers to all the questions above, but I can
tell you in retrospect what was important to Debbie and me in our
marriage after Cammie's death.

It's hard to be supportive of your spouse when you can barely
support yourself.

When you find out your child has died, something in you dies
too. Something dies in your spouse at the same time, but that is hard
to remember and it is hard to support your spouse when you think
you need to be on life support yourself. You find out you are numb.
You start asking the "whys," the "what ifs." Why did this happen?
What could I have done to prevent it? Who caused it? What caused
it? These are all questions you are asking yourself, and your spouse

is going through the same thing simultaneously. It was just difficult to breathe. I love Debbie as much as life itself, but it was hard to consider her thoughts when I was so devastated. My daughter was dead and that was all I could think about . . . but her daughter was dead also.

After weaving your way through the myriad of details . . . when to have a service, where to have a service, what the service needs to look like and be like, who will be involved, the type of casket, the burial place, and the logistics of people coming in from out of town . . . After all of these things are taken care of, which is a miracle in itself how all the pieces come together, and you are left alone with just your spouse and no one else there to hold you up, what do you do? How do you support your spouse when you can barely support yourself? It is no wonder that marriages do not survive after the death of a child.

Not blaming one another

A major contributor to our survival was that Debbie and I never blamed one another for what had happened to Cammie. We both felt that we had done everything we knew to do to support her. We had offered her a place and a time to heal. She could not accept the help that we offered, but that was not Debbie's fault or mine and neither one of us blamed the other.

This is not the norm in most marriages. When a child dies, by whatever means or cause, there is often blame being placed on others, especially the spouse. Placing blame can rapidly lead to the destruction of the marriage without some outside help and intervention.

Ours was a marriage that had survived thirty-five years of living together through everything life had thrown at us. In addition to the truly great times and incredible life we had built together, the marriage had survived family crises, life-threatening illnesses, the suicide of my stepfather, the deaths of Debbie's parents by cancer, and Debbie's own survival of breast cancer.

The main reason I think that neither of us could put any part of the blame on the other was the simple fact that each of us loved Cammie so very much. We had an understanding between us just how deep this love was for the both of us. Along with that came the understanding that either one of us would have done anything possible to have saved her life.

Seeing your spouse in pain and being understanding of their pain—they are hurting too.

I had never been in more pain. I felt like my heart had been ripped out of my body. The pain was excruciating and it would not go away. It was a consuming type of pain that took charge of every aspect of my life. The pain took control of my life and my thoughts. I looked around and there was Deb going through the same thing, suffering the same pain which was controlling her as well.

Normally this would be the time when we would rush to one another's aid, but we were both disabled. It is hard to understand how much pain your spouse is experiencing when you are barely able to survive yourself. You are spending so much energy surviving your own pain that it is hard be understanding of someone else's pain, even when that someone is one you love so much. However, that is exactly what you have to do and that is exactly what happened.

I have never felt more loved by Debbie. She was there to support me in my pain and let me support her in hers. That may sound like double talk, but it is not. We were there for one another. When all the crowds were gone and we were left alone, we truly were there for one another and understood one another's pain.

Communication

Communication is important in any marriage, but when a child dies, the need for communication increases exponentially because of the stress placed upon the marriage. Debbie and I are no exception. Even though we have a strong marriage and communicate about all aspects of our lives, we had not been down this road before. Our need for communication was greater than ever.

One of the things we did that was so important was making time to communicate with each other. Every Wednesday evening Debbie would give me a list of things to talk about or questions to ask of Carmen during our counseling sessions. On Thursday evening, after spending two hours with Carmen, I would come home and Debbie and I would discuss the entire session. We would stay up until twelve or one o'clock discussing and talking about what I had just spent two or three hours talking about. Now this may sound strange to some people, but this was of major importance to our marriage and to our healing.

We not only made time to communicate, but we truly listened to one another. Listening, some say, is a lost skill. We both spent a lot of time truly listening to the other person's wants and needs and alerting each other about our concerns. When Debbie was giving me things to talk to Carmen about or questions to ask Carmen, it was because of her concern and her deep love for me. Debbie saw things she was concerned about that she thought I needed to talk about with someone other than her, and she also knew I was having difficulty concentrating and remembering. This truly was Debbie's loving way of helping me seek help.

Debbie knew I needed help. At the same time, she also knew she could not be my therapist. She, as well as other friends, lovingly communicated my need for professional help. She had never seen me hurting so badly. She had never seen me not able to function, and she was not only concerned, but also frightened. She communicated this to me with a great deal of finesse and an enormous amount of love in her heart. This illustrates communication in a marriage at its finest. This demonstrates being honest and open with each other because our very lives depended on it. She could not just love me through this; she knew I needed professional help.

When you say your wedding vows, you vow to be together for better or for worse. By this time in our marriage, Debbie and I had been through my uncle's suicide, my stepfather's suicide, both of her parents' deaths, and her own breast cancer survival. If this is not a list of the worst, I don't know what is, but the death of a child, the death of our child was the worst thing either of us had ever experienced. I believe this is the worst thing that can happen to a married couple. It takes a lot of love, a lot of understanding, a lot of listening, and a lot of time just holding one another without a single word being said for a marriage to survive. We vowed to be together for better or for worse. We have survived the worst.

Debbie and I are committed to each other and committed to our marriage. We always have been, but an event like this can and often does put a lot of marriages in danger. I am thankful that we had done the hard work before this event happened . . . the listening, the communicating, the understanding, the being honest with one another . . . that makes a marriage not only work, but also enables it to withstand tragedy.

As I said earlier in the book, when this event happened, when my daughter died, I was mad at God. I think this is a fairly normal reaction, asking how this could happen, why this happened, but I also gave you my opinion that we have a God that permits us to get mad at him and still understands and forgives us. Through all of this we both continued to seek God, together and individually. We continued to go to church and were faithful about our prayer time. As I said earlier in the book, prayer is important, especially at a time like this; but I still believe prayer changes *us*, not the mind of God. Prayer opened us up to one another . . . to each of our individual needs. Another theory I have about prayer is that when a married couple seeks God together, the closer they are drawn to God, the closer they subsequently are drawn to each other. So instead of the tragedy causing us to grow apart, it has actually brought us closer together and strengthened our marriage. Another gift!

CHAPTER 36

COMMUNICATE

Carmen

"If God be for us, who can be against us?"
Romans 8:31 KJV

Larry and Debbie had been married for many years at the time Cammie died. They had supported one another through many good times and many difficult times, but the death of Cammie was the most difficult blow they had ever had to cope with as a couple, and it came following all of the other deaths in their lives. It came following multiple family suicidal deaths, cancer, divorce, separation from children, and deaths of parents. Debbie and Larry were strong and had a strong marriage and a strong faith. They had had a wonderful and prosperous life as well. But the death of Cammie brought them to the edge. Sometimes there is a straw that can break the camel's back. The good thing was that they knew it, particularly Debbie. Debbie was hurting badly, but had a little more energy than Larry. She could see him on the edge. She knew he was on the edge and she knew that she must get him some help this time.

Debbie has the best intuition of anyone I have ever known. She is actually known by her friends for her excellent intuition. Her intuition told her that she could support herself and could support Larry if Larry had some professional help. Her intuition told her that she could not be the only support this time around. This blow was too severe. Her intuition told her that they were able to get through the other crises with each other and help from God. Her intuition told her that she must do whatever was needed so that her husband could survive and have the care that he needed and deserved. One of the major ways that Debbie supported Larry was through insisting that he get guidance and counseling regarding the death of Cammie and then through encouraging him to do the work and therapy that would be necessary if he was to survive the suicide of their child.

Larry supported Debbie once he was stabilized emotionally. He listened, shared what he was learning in therapy and encouraged her to talk as much as she needed to. The more healing Larry experienced, the more he could support Debbie. As they both healed, the more they could support one another.

Not blaming one another

One of the common occurrences one finds in grief is blame and guilt. They are almost automatic. They are not rational, and they are deadly to a marriage if they are not expressed and addressed early on in the grief process. The reason they are not rational is because our minds automatically take us to these places and try to make sense of something that is not logical. Suicide is not logical. Suicide is irrational. Suicide is the loss of hope in someone who is struggling, but our minds try to tell us that we caused the problem, we could have stopped it, someone else caused it, and someone else could have stopped it. These are irrational thoughts on our part and if we go down that road of irrational blame we will only wind up feeling victimized. It is important, however, to learn from our experiences and with so many suicides in the Simons family, Larry wanted to learn. Larry wanted to stop this pattern. Larry and Debbie wanted to genuinely learn if there was anything they had done to contribute to the suicide of Cammie or if there was anything they could have done to prevent it. They knew in their hearts that they would have done anything to prevent Cammie from committing suicide.

And so Larry and Debbie did what is called "processing" the events prior to and surrounding Cammie's death by suicide. Processing simply means talking about the events in a logical, realistic, and rational way. The process is simple, but often very difficult and painful to do; however, the outcome of this process can give great relief and prevent further injury to the grievers. Processing can mean the difference between successful healing for grievers and lifelong agony and repeated self-doubt regarding the death of a loved one.

The discussion Larry, Debbie, and I had involved questions about responsibility, awareness, facts, and culpability. It takes great courage to look at one's own behavior and the behavior of a child prior to a death by suicide because the answers are unknown and the fear is great. Debbie and Larry were fearless in their discussion individually and as a couple, and my job was to be as honest and rational with them as possible. Larry and Debbie learned that they had no culpability in the death of Cammie. They learned that they had done everything possible to help Cammie once they learned about her illness. They had offered her refuge, medical and psychological help, love, caring, and vocational and financial guidance. They learned that Cammie had kept the abusive treatment by her husband a secret from her parents for many years. They learned that human beings are not mind readers and cannot know things about which they are not informed. Larry was clear about what he would have done had he known about the abuse, but he had to accept the fact that he was not informed.

After reviewing everything they had done once they knew about Cammie's illnesses and realizing they had done everything humanly possible to help her, they felt better. They also had to realize that Cammie was an adult and that an adult cannot be controlled no matter how much they had wanted to control the situation. They learned the painful truth that many survivors of suicide learn after the fact, and that is that if a person has lost all hope and is intent on committing suicide, the suicide is all but impossible to prevent.

They learned that with all of Cammie's illnesses, the imbalance in her hormones and chemicals, the abusive situation she had lived in for a number of years, that she came to a point of pain and hopelessness that, in her mind, could only be stopped one way, and that way was suicide.

Debbie and Larry had the courage to look at these facts and realities alone and together and the strength to accept that they could not rationally accept blame for the death of their daughter. They learned that it was neither rational nor realistic to blame themselves for something over which they had no control. This may sound obvious to anyone fortunate enough not to have experienced a suicide in his or her family, but for actual survivors it is a very difficult thing to do. Even Debbie and Larry had to continue to work hard to deal with the repeated triggers in their minds to accept guilt and blame for Cammie's death. But once they learned the truth of the situation, they were armed with truth and knowledge to be vigilant and fight these triggers, and they continued to fight them until they eventually began to diminish over time.

Getting clear on guilt and blame is one is one of the most critical factors in the longevity and stability of a marriage following the death of a loved one.

Communication

Debbie and Larry had exceptional communication throughout their marriage and continued their communication throughout the grieving process. They talked about everything and left no stone unturned. They understood and accepted that irritability and edginess were part of the process and allowed for these occurrences in one another and didn't take them personally.

They shared their breakthroughs, their vulnerabilities, their sadness, pain, and tears, along with their sweet memories. As Larry and Debbie continued to share their thoughts and feelings daily, they were also preventing resentments from building up and sabotaging their marriage. Their communication was helping them support one another in the present and was also a preventative strategy for future conflict based on unspoken issues.

CHAPTER 37

THE JOURNEY TO WHOLENESS
Larry

"We make a living by what we get,
but we make a life by what we give."
Winston Churchill

Moving from success to significance . . . Cammie's life as a school teacher was very successful and very significant. Cammie was a very talented teacher and her students and other faculty members loved her. What she accomplished in the lives of her students was truly significant. Most often in life, success dies with you, but significance lives on. The hearts and lives that Cammie touched will continue to live on. As several of her students said, she made learning fun. What greater accolade can a teacher receive? A little bit of Cammie will remain forever in the minds and hearts of her students.

Cammie's life has helped me move from success toward significance in my own life. I am much more concerned about what I can do to give back, what I can do to make a difference in someone's life. How can I help? How can I touch and change lives? I know I cannot do it the way Cammie did it, but I think because of her example I can and will make a difference in people's lives. I want to help people in grief to be able to see the joy in life again. I want to help people in grief see that it is possible to move through grief back to wholeness. I want to help people learn to see and understand that life is a gift, that having the person they are grieving for was a gift. To be able to say thank you each and every day for the gift of their own lives and for the gift of their loved ones. To be able to get out of bed each and every morning saying thank you, thank you, thank you, until the hair on the back of their necks is standing up because they are not only able to say thank you, but they are able to feel the gratitude, feel the joy, understand the gift. That is recovery.

I want to help people understand the importance attitude plays in every area of their lives. To understand that attitude plays an important role in any recovery, whether it is in grief recovery or in addiction recovery. It all starts with the right attitude.

Debbie thinks that some people get stuck in grief. The fact is a lot of people do get stuck in grief. They feel like if they start moving on with life again they are not honoring their loved ones. I think getting stuck in grief is the worst possible thing that can happen because it is not about the person who died. Getting stuck in grief is all about me, whereas honoring my loved one is all about them.

Moving through the grief back to wholeness is a healthy thing to do. It may be the hardest work one has ever done, but it's worth all the time and the work. I feel that healing, returning to wholeness is the best possible way to honor our loved ones.

For me, this entire experience of moving through the grief back to wholeness has been an incredible paradigm shift. Let me explain what I mean. Cammie died. She is no longer in this world in a physical form. Cammie is now in the present heaven. Her death shook me to the core. In the course of moving through the grief I had to do a great deal of self-examination. I found some things about my life that needed changing and I was able to change them right away. Other things I am still working on, but the experience has changed my entire life. It has changed how I will spend the last third of my life.

Cammie's life ended in the physical form in this world, but her life really did not end. She just changed forms. I thought for a while that Cammie's death was going to end my life, but it didn't. By working through the grief, by doing the hard work that it takes to return to wholeness, I have become a different person. I am able to look at life in a totally different way. My values have changed. My character has changed. My priorities have changed.

For the first time in my life I am able to clearly see my life's true purpose. Before Cammie's death my purpose was to be successful. To me that meant being in the top of my field and earning the income associated with that. It was about building personal wealth and being able to leave a financial legacy for my family. As important as that is, that is not life's purpose.

Now I understand my purpose in life. I truly believe each of us is put on this earth for a reason. I believe God put us on this earth to be in fellowship with him and serve him. I believe the way we serve God is through serving other people. That is how I intend on living out this last third of my earthly life. The paradigm shift is that it took something as horrendous as my daughter's death for me to truly understand this.

I remember Carmen saying to me in the beginning of our time together during our counseling sessions, that I would grow through this process. I still remember how angry it made me feel for someone to say that I would receive growth because of my daughter's death. But that was not what Carmen was saying at all. The growth came not from my daughter's death, but from truly understanding my daughter's life. I grew from being grateful for having the opportunity to be her father. I grew from having the opportunity to understand Cammie as a gift.

Before Cammie's death, I thought my retirement years would be spent using my tools to help people grow financially, to grow in the business world. Now I still plan on using my tools, but through this process, through Carmen's counseling and guidance, I now see these tools as a way to help people in grief and in recovery. I don't know what the future holds, but my prayer to God is to use me as a tool to do his will and serve his people. To help hurting, grieving people be restored to wholeness. To help hurting, grieving people understand the gift, the gift of gratitude, the gift of love.

CHAPTER 38

MOVING FROM SUCCESS TO SIGNIFICANCE

Carmen

"It's about the journey—mine and yours—and the lives we can touch, the legacy we can leave, and the world we can change for the better."
Tony Dungy[6]

Although I did not know Larry prior to the death of Cammie, I could not help but be struck by the fact that Larry was a changed man because of the life and death of his child. I had not heard many fathers describe their child as being their hero. I wanted to try to understand his perceptions and his responses to her life and death.

Larry kept saying that Cammie's life was very significant. This struck me because by all standard measures of success, Larry was highly successful professionally, financially, and socially. He was also happily married and had been for thirty-five years. He had two children and four grandchildren whom he loved dearly. And yet Larry revered his daughter for her significance. I asked him what he meant. Financially, socially, and personally Cammie had struggled and had not outwardly achieved the heights that Larry appeared to have attained, and yet he revered Cammie. What was this all about?

I kept asking questions to try to understand Larry's perception of his child. The answer lay in his understanding of the impact Cammie had on others as a teacher. Larry himself had mentored many young men in business over the years and had had an important impact on their lives and their success in business. But to Larry this paled in comparison to the impact Cammie had had on the lives of dozens and dozens of children over the span of her career as a teacher.

As he told me the story of the response of Cammie's students at the visitation, telling him that Cammie had "made learning fun," I realized that he was touched very deeply inside. This response had resonated deep inside Larry at a level not reached previously.

It appeared that something in Larry revered, respected, and valued the achievement of his child to touch the hearts, minds, and spirits of children in ways that were profound and spiritual. I believe he came to the realization that Cammie had made the most valuable contribution that a human being can make while alive on earth no matter the length of time present here. It seemed that he valued the spiritual contribution she had made above those that were financial or materialistic in nature.

Something seemed to have changed in Larry on many levels when he made this realization. It became something on which to focus following Cammie's death. He had a choice to continue to focus on her death and the tragedy of her suicide. He also now had a choice to focus on the contribution his child had made to the world through her work making the lives of special needs children a little easier. When given the choice on which to focus for the remainder of his life, the choice was clear. Larry chose to focus on the love he had for his child and the significant contribution she had made to the world while she was here. This one decision would affect the direction of Larry's life for the remainder of his years.

On another level, experiencing the significance of Cammie's contribution to children inspired Larry to want to contribute something more than money, prestige, and influence to the world. He now wanted to contribute something more significant through the inspiration of the life of his own child. His daughter had now become his hero and he wanted to be more like her in the last third of his life. He wasn't sure how that would be done, but he knew he liked the feeling.

The idea of making a spiritually significant contribution to help make the lives of people a little easier or better began to inspire Larry. He began sharing his story of recovery with others including grieving children, teens, and adults. He began writing about his recovery and how he had survived and was actually beginning to thrive again in spite of all of the tragedy. I enjoyed watching Larry giving hope to others in grief and inspiring them to continue on their road to recovery. He began to attract a following of people who wanted to learn how to survive the tragedies in their own lives. As I watched I began to realize that Cammie's gift of teaching others and touching lives in a significant way appeared to have been passed on to Larry. Spiritually, it seemed that Cammie had passed on this amazing gift to her father. Cammie had given the gift of helping others in a significant way to her father and he had accepted it with profound appreciation and great joy. No greater gift could have been left for Larry than this one. Cammie left her father the greatest gift of all, the gift of helping and healing God's children.

Larry considers this the greatest gift he has ever received and cherishes it highly. He is very thankful to Cammie for, although she is gone and not present on a physical plane, her gift lives on in her father and he is sharing it in her honor with those God sends his way.

To God be the glory.

AFTERWORD

Dear Reader,

If this book was meaningful to you and helped you in any way we invite you to contact us. We welcome your stories about your *journey to wholeness.* Please tell us about the tools you used and how they were helpful to you.

If your life was touched in any way by Larry's daughter, Cammie Simons, during her lifetime as a friend, colleague, student, parent, or in any other capacity, we would love to hear from you and we welcome your stories. You may have known Cammie as Cammie Simons, Cammie Woodell or Cammie Springer.

Please send your stories to Larry and Carmen. Larry Simons is available for speaking engagements and seminars. For contact information please visit our website: **www.theattitudeforum.com**

May our God continue to bless you on your journey to wholeness.

RECOMMENDED READING LIST

1. *The Holy Bible*

2. *Good Grief*
    Granger E. Westberg

3. *Tracks of a Fellow Struggler*
    John R. Claypool

4. *The Power of Positive Thinking*
    Dr. Norman Vincent Peale

5. *The Courage to Grieve*
    Judy Tatelbaum

6. *I Wasn't Ready to Say Goodbye*
    Brook Noel & Pamela D. Blair

7. *As a Man Thinketh*
    James Allen

8. *The Last Lecture*
    Randy Pausch

9. *Think and Grow Rich*
    Napoleon Hill

10. *The Greatest Salesman in the World*
        Og Mandino

11. *The Greatest Miracle in the World*
        Og Mandino

12. *Same Kind of Different as Me*
        Ron Hall & Denver Moore

13. *Younger Next Year*
        Crowley & Lodge

14. *Your Relationship with God*
        Dr. Gary Smalley

15. *How to Stop Worrying & Start Living*
        Dale Carnegie

16. *Success through a Positive Mental Attitude*
        W. Clement Stone

17. *The Road Less Traveled*
        M. Scott Peck M.D.

18. *90 Minutes in Heaven*
        Don Piper

19. *The New Psycho-Cybernetics*
        Maxwell Maltz M.D.

20. *You Only Die Once*
        Margie Jenkins

21. *The Science of Getting Rich*
        Wallace D. Wattles

REFERENCES

(5) The Episcopal Church, *The Book of Common Prayer*, (New York, NY: The Church Pension Fund, 1979)

(6) Tony Dungy, *Quiet Strength,* (Carol Stream: Tyndale House, 2007)

(4) Napoleon Hill, *Think and Grow Rich*, (Los Angeles: Highroads Media, 2004)

(2) C. S. Lewis, *A Grief Observed,* (New York, NY: Harper Collins, 1989)

(1) Joel Osteen, *Your Best Life Now*, (New York, NY: Warner Faith, 2004)

(3) Carol Staudacher, *A Time to Grieve*, (San Francisco: Harper 1994)

ABOUT THE AUTHORS

Larry Simons

Author Larry Simons rose from humble beginnings in Texas to become a highly successful and respected salesman in the corporate world. Beloved by family, friends, and colleagues, Larry is known for his eternal optimism, personal integrity, positive attitude and unwavering faith. However, unknown to many, Larry is the survivor of four family deaths by suicide including those of his father, uncle, stepfather and precious daughter, Cammie. Journey to Wholeness is the inspirational story of his journey from unimaginable sorrow and brokenness to finding significance, meaning, and happiness in his life again. Larry shares his strategies and tools so you can learn the skills for what may be the most important journey of your life. Larry and his wife Debbie live in Austin, Texas.

Carmen DiNino Alspach

Author Carmen DiNino Alspach is the Johns Hopkins University trained therapist who assisted Larry Simons in his grief recovery. As a Licensed Professional Counselor and Licensed Chemical Dependency Counselor specializing in recovery from profound grief, addictions and trauma, Carmen has shared strategies for transcending agonizing pain and sorrow with her clients in private, public and military settings and welcomes the opportunity to share this important information with readers. Respected by her many clients, Carmen utilizes her unique perspective as both a survivor of suicide herself and as a trained clinician to help others understand suicidal ideation from prevention to aftermath to recovery. Carmen and her husband Rick live just outside Austin, Texas.